WHAT DID I DO LAST NIGHT?

To the Monk

WHAT DID I DO LAST NIGHT?

a drunkard's tale

TOM SYKES

EBURY
PRESS

1 3 5 7 9 10 8 6 4 2

This edition published in 2008

First published in Great Britain in 2007 by Ebury Press,
an imprint of Ebury Publishing

A Random House Group Company

The Random House Group Limited Reg. No. 954009

Addresses for companies within the Random House Group can be found at
www.randomhouse.co.uk

A CIP catalogue record for this book is available from the British Library

Penguin Random House is committed to a sustainable future for
our business, our readers and our planet. This book is made from
Forest Stewardship Council® certified paper.

Printed and bound in Great Britain by Clays Ltd, Elcograf S.p.A.

ISBN 9780091916558

To buy books by your favourite authors and register for offers visit
www.rbooks.co.uk

Excerpt on pages 138–139 courtesy of the *New York Observer*.

ACKNOWLEDGEMENTS

A giant thank you to everyone who has made this possible. Firstly, my family: my incredible wife, Sasha; my mother, Valerie; my sisters, Lucy, Plum and Alice; my brothers, Fred and Josh; my father, Mark; and my brothers-in-law, Euan, Chris and Toby. My work colleagues; Chris Wilson, for continuing to be the greatest man in the known world for a wild night out in New York City; and Paula Froelich, for introducing me to my US editor Leigh Haber in the first place. Thanks to my friends, especially Rupert, Robin, Neil, Simon, Steve, Olly, Tom Craig, "Frank", "James", Helen and Alex for letting me use their stories and helping me remember all the nonsense we got up to. Thanks are also due to Luke Janklow, Tif Loehnis, Andrew Goodfellow, Tracey Westmoreland and Eddie B. And thanks to James Frey for the importance of the following statements: Everything in this book is absolutely true, although sequences have been rearranged and conversations recreated, often on the basis of subsequent interviews. The names "James", "Frank", "Brad", "Matthew Mole", "Ben White" and "Greg Davidson" are pseudonyms.

PROLOGUE

IT WAS SOMEWHERE past midnight and I was standing at the bar in Siberia, complaining that my martini seemed a bit weak.

"Patrick," I called out over the long wooden bar, "Did you let the ice melt in this or something?"

"What?" sighed Patrick, the long-suffering barman. He pushed his long hair back from his face as he walked towards me, framed by a pyramid of glowing liquor bottles stacked behind him. "What's the matter, Tom?"

"It's this martini," I grumbled. "It doesn't seem to have any kick in it."

"No kick! It's pure vodka, man. That's what a martini is. A martini *can't be* weak."

"Maybe the ice melted."

"You want me to make you another?"

"No, no," I muttered. "It's fine. Whatever."

My best friend, Chris Wilson, who I worked with on

Page Six, the gossip column at the *New York Post*, was standing next to me at the bar.

"I find it's advisable to drink only pre-packaged alcohol at Siberia," he said, taking a pull on his stubby bottle of Heineken.

He had a point. Siberia, a windowless cave located in the New York district of Hell's Kitchen, on the corner of 40th Street and 9th Avenue, was no cocktail lounge. It was, however, widely reckoned to be the best dive bar in New York, with a wealth of idiosyncratic detail, like an old porcelain toilet slung by chains from the roof above the serving area with a blow-up sex doll stuffed head first into the bowl, and two vintage Harley-Davidsons parked in the middle of the bar. The wooden chipboard floor was coated with years of drinks spillage, which had evaporated to leave a mystery viscous detritus the colour and texture of molasses which was impossible to get off your clothes if you fell over. Siberia had no sign outside, just a small red bulb winking into the night. It all added up to a dubiously charming kind of appeal.

Anything went at Siberia, thanks in large part to its nineteen-stone, goatee-sporting owner, Tracey Westmoreland, who was just now striding through the swing door bringing a blast of icy December air with him. I was always pleased to see Tracey, not least because he made sure his friends, especially those who wrote about nightlife for a living, drank for free.

He gave me a bear hug, too tight, verging on painful, as usual.

"Patrick," he called over the bar, and pointed at me and Chris, "These guys are on a full scholarship."

"Cheers mate," I said to Tracey as he disappeared off to the other end of the bar. Then, to Patrick, my head spinning now, "Let me have another one of your martinis. Can you try and make it a little stronger this time?"

Patrick shrugged, his palms flat up in the air in despair.

The next two hours didn't come back to me until the next day. I walked around the bar, bitching about the insufficient potency of Patrick's martinis to anyone who would listen to me, my feet sticking to the gluey floor like a moonwalker struggling with gravity. Then I was climbing over the counter, trying to get Patrick to switch off the jukebox and put an Ozzy Osbourne CD on the stereo behind the bar. I had been sent the CD at work and had been carrying it in my pocket all night.

Patrick must have put it on because the next thing was that I was dancing on the low stage that ran round the back wall of the room to Ozzy. Coloured lights were dazzling my eyes. I picked up an old metal chair and began playing air guitar to the song, *Paranoid*. As the crowd roared, the world shifted half a degree, and suddenly, I *was* Ozzy Osbourne, performing *Paranoid* live, to a sold-out crowd of thousands.

I gave my fans the rock salute, and yelled, "Come on!" They screamed back their appreciation. But how could I, Ozzy Osbourne, take this performance to the next level?

The next thing I knew, I was twenty foot up in the air, looking down on the stage. Right in the middle, bathed in pulsing orange and green light stood a guy in a Paul Smith shirt and APC jeans. He was swinging a chair high up in the air and bringing it down with astounding force, over and over again on an old Eighties video-arcade game, a Pac-Man machine that looked like a table; competitors sat on either side of it. Glass was flying, smoke was pouring out of the caved-in screen. Everything was happening in slow motion, it looked like Siberia had been smothered in treacle.

What was going on? Who was that guy?

The man lifted the chair up above his head again. His hair was flying back with the momentum, his eyes were bloodshot red and his wide-open mouth was letting out a frenzied, furious, blood-curdling scream.

That was when I realised, with horror, that it was me. I floated sickeningly above the stage, disembodied, watching myself flail drunkenly among the glass and the metal and the smoke.

If that was me then what was I doing up here? Was I about to die?

What had I become?

1

-5214 DAYS

MY SCHOOL HAD A PUB, and I was pacing urgently across a cobbled courtyard towards it. It was the first day of the winter term, the new school year, the first day I was allowed to drink there, and I was late.

At Eton College you were allowed in the school bar, which was actually called Tap, at sixteen. The school got round the licensing laws by claiming Tap was a private social club. Technically you were only allowed two pints of beer. In reality, and presumably without Eton's knowledge, you had to fall over before the locals who worked the pumps would cut you off. The beer at Tap was subsidised, so it was cheaper than the pubs we drank at during the holidays in London.

Tap was just one more unique oddity of being a student at Eton. Some of the other, less enjoyable, idiosyncrasies included wearing a tail suit to lessons every day, playing sports unknown outside the school walls (the field game, the wall game and Eton fives), and having to learn a whole new language, where teachers were "beaks" and new boys were "tits". Fortunately the ancient tradition of having to run errands for older boys, known as "fagging", had recently been abolished. Tourists and parents considered these anachronisms quaint and charming. Three years in, I just thought it was normal.

Tap – which was open from 4pm to 6.10pm on Tuesdays and Thursdays and from 4pm–6pm on Saturdays, when there was also "late Tap" from 8pm to 10.15pm for prefects – was a privilege reserved for the senior boys in their final two years. For once I couldn't wait to get back to school, although my delight was not only down to the promise of Tap.

Home was hell at the moment. Two years earlier – when I was fourteen – my mercurial father had abandoned my mother and his six children and run off to the South of France to become a born-again playboy. He never sent my mum any money to support his children, and as a result of all this my mother had suffered a major nervous breakdown. Then the idyllic farmhouse in Kent where I had grown up, surrounded by nut orchards and rolling fields, and which actually belonged to my grandmother, who lived there with us, had been sold to pay off my parents' debts. My mum was chronically broke and still in bed most of the time, my grandmother and various friends and relatives were paying my school fees and home was now a rented cottage on my uncle's farm in Surrey. My older twin sisters, Plum and Lucy, had left home to go to university and drama school respectively. Alice, who was two years older than me, had finished school and taken off to Europe on an extended vacation. My younger brother Fred was seven, a study in baffled melancholy, and my baby brother Josh, who was three now, had recently been hospitalised after eating handfuls of my mother's anti-depressants in what I perceived to be a precocious suicide attempt.

I scratched my leg under the itchy pinstriped wool trousers, my steps jarring my bones as I raced towards Tap. I was relieved that Josh had recovered, of course, but I kept wondering whether if he had died that would have been enough to get my parents back together. As things stood, the Sykes family was well and truly fucked.

Still, I was going to Tap for the first time and the next couple of hours were going to be just fine. None of my friends at school really knew quite how desperate my home situation was. They knew about my dad leaving, of course, and that was embarrassing enough, but I hadn't made anyone familiar with the miserable updated details.

I pushed through the swing doors into a scene of pandemonium. Hundreds of over-privileged sixteen-year-old boys were waving £50 notes and cheque books at the bar staff and screaming for more and more alcohol. I pushed my way to the bar through a sea of black tail coats.

"A pint of lager please, Mrs Cripps," I shouted at the bar woman. I already knew her name because in the mornings she worked in the tuck shop which backed on to Tap, selling us bacon rolls.

I grabbed my pint off the bar and wriggled out of the crowd, looking around for my friends. They were sitting in a gang of about twenty, on a leather banquette that skirted the corner of the room, grinning like maniacs at their pints. I managed to sit down next to my friend Ben White.

"Psycho! Where have you been?" he asked. Ben was well over six feet tall and built like an international rugby player.

"Harrison made me rake the bloody leaves off his lawn again," I said, swallowing beer as fast as I could and explaining why I had arrived at Tap half an hour after the opening bell. David Harrison was my housemaster, and I seemed to spend most of my free time clearing leaves off his lawn as punishment for one transgression or another. In his eyes, I had started off the term as badly as ever by not unpacking all my cases properly and leaving my room in a mess.

The man was as fanatical about his garden as he was loathed by me and my friends. These two defining facts about Dr Death, as we called him, would conflate gloriously the following term when two boys in our house crept out in the middle of the night and weed-killed a giant cock and balls on his prized half-moon lawn.

"Typical," said Ben, shouting in my ear to make himself heard above the hubbub. "That's so unfair. Today of all days." Then he looked around at the basic surroundings of Tap with all the excitement of a new intimate and said, "This is bloody amazing isn't it? Is that your first pint?"

"Yep," I said, "But I've nearly finished it. I'm going to

get another in a minute."

"I'm on my third," he said. "If I give you the money can you get me one to line up for when this one is finished?"

He had hardly made a dent in the drink he had, but I said, "Indeed". Indeed was my new favourite word. "Lager?"

"No. Newcastle Brown. In a jug." I stood up, trying not to let on I didn't know what he meant.

I fought my way back to the bar and ordered a Newcastle Brown for Ben and copied him, getting one for myself instead of a lager. "In jugs, please, Mrs Cripps," I said, hopefully. The beers were slammed on the bar in fat, handled, windowed glasses, that were easy to carry through the melee.

"This is great, isn't it?" I said for about the fiftieth time, as I sat down next to Ben again. "Can you believe how cheap it is? I can't believe we get cheap beer."

After two more pints, my head was spinning. The place looked like a cross between a tuck shop and a gin mill. The bathrooms stank of vomit. Boys in tail suits were sitting in stupefied dazes all around the edge of the room, long hair flopping over their pale, pimpled faces. I saw my friend Gerry, who was in the year above me.

"How many pints have you had?" I shouted.

"Seven," he burped beerily. "Usually I forget how many I've had, but today I've been drawing them on my hand so that I won't." He proudly stuck his hand out, covered in inky caricatures of the squat beer glasses Ben had asked to be served in. I clapped him on the back, deeply impressed. One day, I swore, I would be able to drink that much.

At 6.10pm Tap closed. This was so the boys could get back to their boarding houses in time for quiet hour, the study period that started at 6.15pm every night and lasted till dinner at 7.30. Today, there wasn't going to be much work going on.

I trooped back to my boarding house with Ben and my eight other housemates. One good thing about Eton was that everyone got their own room, complete with a desk and a bed on hinges that you had to strap the mattress down on and fold up into the wall every morning before breakfast. You could decorate your room however you liked. My walls were covered in Pink Floyd posters and ethnic-print drapes.

I had drunk four pints and my head was spinning, but I resisted the temptation to pull my bed down from the wall and lie on it, in case Harrison came barging in to check up on me. I didn't want to do any more leaf sweeping. I sat at the wooden desk in the corner of the room by the window with my hands over my eyes.

Eton was a confusing place. Just six months previously I had been "rusticated" (suspended from school, as in, "sent home to the country") for five days after Ben and I had been caught buying vodka in Windsor. Now I was allowed to drink – but I would be in big trouble if Harrison discovered how drunk I was.

Getting money for drinking sessions was no problem.

Although my dad never supported my mother, he was in the habit of sending me occasional but extravagant cheques from his hidey-hole in the South of France several times a year. They were often accompanied by bizarre jokes or cartoons. One that I remember said, "I went to the theatre the other night and the following rhyme occurred to me. 'If Federico Garcia Lorca/ Had been born a pig/ He would have been called Federico Garcia Porca.'" In another letter, a cartoon showed a smug gentleman orbiting the earth, leaning back in an armchair with a glass of port and a cigar, his slippered feet stretched out on a stool. The earth was exploding. My dad had written the caption, "The End of The World Viewed in Comfort" underneath.

The one thing I could guarantee was that my dad's letters would never address the one thing that mattered. Whenever I wrote letters which demanded to know why he had left my mum, I would usually receive a short note in return, saying something like, "It became impossible for your mother and I to continue living together," with a check for £500, sometimes even £1,000.

Although I tried not to, I missed my dad. He was an incredible storyteller and raconteur. When I was little, one of my favourite games was getting him to list his jobs. He had been an avocado farmer in East Timor and a racing driver in Australia. In the Vietnam War he had sold blankets to the Vietcong. He had started a nightclub (The Wag in Soho), run lucrative illegal gambling operations in England and Australia, reported on the French Foreign Legion spearing babies to doorposts with bayonets in Algeria, and even smuggled weapons to support the Arabs in their insurrection against the French in North Africa. Often, he would hint darkly that he had killed a man. When we drove down the country lanes from our house to the nearest town, Sevenoaks, he would sneak up behind pheasants in the car, sound his horn and then whack into them with the windscreen, with us children screaming with excitement on the back seat. We'd pick up the dead birds on the way home, once they had stopped twitching, and my mum's old nanny Winnie, who still worked for my granny, would pluck them and cook them for dinner. Being with Dad was thrilling.

The last time I really saw my father was on Remembrance Day, November 11. It was 1988 and I was fourteen. Dad drove to Eton with my sister Plum for the service on the morning of Remembrance Day – he was driving her to Oxford where she was studying.

The service sticks in my memory because it was a weekday, twenty minutes in the chapel before school -- basically an assembly with prayers. Parents never came to these services. They came to the hour-long services on a Sunday instead. I kept wondering for days afterwards why Dad had come to chapel at Eton mid-week.

I have seen my father many times since then, but that was the last time I saw him before everything changed. Even on that day I had a sense that things were changing. My dad looked, older, fatter, different somehow. I noticed that his hair was dyed a lighter brown than usual. Plum looked older too – but in a more positive way. Plum had been shy, serious and nervous as a teenager. Since leaving school and going to Oxford that year she had become newly confident and her whole presence was transformed. She was beautiful; slim, with strong features and long brown hair. Because Plum was with my dad they were seated at the front of the chapel, on a raised dais reserved for dignitaries. I could just see the Lower Master thinking, "Yes, yes, that's a fine idea! Let's seat this girl somewhere prominent, somewhere all our female-deprived boys can see a beautiful young woman! That'll be some first-class entertainment for them!"

I can't remember anything of the service beyond their presence, or much of the weeks that followed. But soon after there was a four-day holiday, Short Leave. When I got home to the farmhouse in Kent, the horrible truth emerged.

My father had sent nearly all the valuable furniture, paintings and antiques in our house to be "restored". All his suits had gone to the "dry cleaner". I can imagine him scooping up every last two-piece out of his cupboard, "Time to get everything cleaned!" and loading up all the suits into the car and driving them away. Then he packed his few remaining belongings and announced he was off to the South of France on a business trip.

The suits never returned from the dry cleaner. And although a few pieces of furniture were sent back, the paintings were gone for good too. Sometimes, when I visit him these days, I'll see one of the pictures that disappeared from my childhood hanging on his wall, and I'll remember how their removal left nothing but very neat squares of very clean paint underneath.

"You're the man of the house, now," my grandmother told me, and I nodded dumbly in agreement, baffled at how quickly my world had fallen apart.

That Christmas, my father came back for a few days, but the knowledge of his ongoing affairs in London became too much for my mother to bear. In the end, it was she who told him to leave.

When I got back to school in the new year of 1989, I was ashamed to admit to my friends that my family had broken up. I was fourteen and I didn't want to be an object of pity. I felt like a fraud in the perfect world of Eton, where everyone else's parents were rich, happy and together. At Eton, broken homes were something that happened to other people.

To make matters even worse, one of the women my father had chosen to have an affair with was a close relative of The Dame, the middle-aged, grey-haired spinster who acted as house matron, and lived in a small upstairs apartment in my boarding house.

She came into my room one night before lights out, sitting on the edge of my bed, in her starched blue uniform, stroking the bedcovers, unable to look me in the eye.

Eventually she said, in her prim Scottish accent, "I know things are difficult at the moment Tom, and I feel terrible because it involves my family."

I just lay there, sitting up in bed, desperately wishing

she would go away because I had hurriedly thrust a copy of *Penthouse* I was perusing down the side of my bed when she walked in.

"It's not your fault," I said.

"Just remember that there are two people in the world who love you," she said.

"I'm not so sure about that," I said, trying not to cry.

She sat on my bed for another long minute, picking the fluff off my blanket. Eventually she stood up. She seemed to be searching for some words that might make it all better. There were none.

"Well, I am sorry," she said. "If you ever want to talk, you know you can come up to my flat any time."

"Yes, ma'am," I said. She got up to leave, gave me a thin smile, and shut the door behind her. I sank into my pillow, groaning with humiliation and shame.

A few days later, on the first weekend of the spring term, I got drunk for the first time on a couple of cans of Special Brew, a viscous lager boasting a formidable alcohol content, which Ben had smuggled into school. A group of four of us drank two cans each in another boy's room. All our rooms were painted a vivid shade of yellow, and this one was no exception, so we covered a bedside lamp with a piece of cloth to "mellow out".

The taste of the beer made me retch a few times, but I got used to it before I was halfway through the can. Ben "shotgunned" his second can, punching a hole in the side with a knife and clamping his lips around the wound. With his head sideways and the beer can held upright, someone else opened the ring pull. Ben drank the contents in a matter of seconds. We all cheered as he let out a giant burp.

I gave shotgunning a go myself with my second can. I had to swallow beer furiously from the moment the ring pull was opened, but the good thing was that I could only taste bubbles because the beer was flowing so fast. Afterwards I felt sick.

It was great.

No one was laughing at me because of my dad anymore. I felt elated that these four guys who I was lying on the floor with, giggling, spinning gently, trusted me enough, liked me enough, to include me. I knew I was drunk and I loved it. In fact, I was already planning how to get some more beer the following weekend.

2

-5100 DAYS

AP WAS A CLEAR improvement on the tuck shop, but it
had its limitations. For starters it was only open for a
few hours a day, which was enough time to get drunk if you
moved fast but not conducive to a really good session.
Secondly, you couldn't smoke at Tap, and I liked to smoke
when I drank. And thirdly I missed the thrill of breaking the
rules. So I carried on going over the bridge to Windsor to
go to the pubs or to buy booze to drink on the playing fields
with whoever I could persuade to accompany me.

You had to be careful not to let on you were an Etonian
in the Windsor pubs. The locals would eye us suspiciously.
We assumed they were itching to hang an Etonian scalp on
their wall.

After being rusticated for buying vodka with Ben, I tried
to purchase my alcohol at unusual locations. One of my
favourite spots was a French wine outlet store called

Bordeaux Direct, located in a refurbished railway arch in Windsor. I cut through the pockets of my overcoat so I could carry two bottles of wine back to school in its lining. I felt so smart, as I grinned good day to the beaks I passed on the street on my way back to my house.

Ben's enthusiasm for hanging out with me had started to wane a little, especially after we had been caught buying the vodka, and my new best friend was another boy in my house called Rupert Neville. Rupert lived near me at home, so we saw each other in the holidays. As well as drinking he also liked smoking cigarettes and gambling on the horses – neither of which was Ben's thing.

Over drinks in a Windsor pub one Saturday afternoon, when we were supposed to be playing rugby, Rupert became conspiratorial.

"Harrison made me move some of his shitty old furniture into the cellar the other day," he said, pushing his big glasses up his nose.

"Oh yeah?" I said, unsurprised. Being corralled into doing your housemaster's menial labour was nothing new.

"Yeah. And I noticed, he keeps his wine down there."

I looked at Rupert intently. "Really? Could we get it?"

"Well, I don't know," Rupert said, stirring his drink – a brandy and ginger ale – thoughtfully and lighting yet another self-rolled cigarette. We both smoked roll-ups. "There's a locked gate in front of it, but it's like a big grid, and some of the wine is near the front."

"And?"

"I think we could reach it."

That was all I needed to hear. The next night, before we went to bed we both set our alarm clocks for three o'clock. When the alarm went off, I silenced it immediately and got out of bed, dressing in a pair of jeans, trainers, and my long overcoat to keep out the cold. I crept down the passageway and met Rupert in the big bathroom on our floor as we had arranged. He was wearing his dark red dressing gown and holding a torch. We gave each other a thumbs-up sign, and then crept down the main stairs of the house in total silence.

The entrance to the cellar was via a small, tightly sprung door, which gave directly on to another set of very steep, narrow stairs. As we tiptoed down them, I tried not to think how much trouble I would be in if I was caught. I would almost certainly be expelled. I should have been being extra careful because just a few months before I had been arrested by the police for riding my sister's motorbike on the roads during the school holidays. I was fifteen – too young to have a licence – and drunk, and the school had found out when I had to go to court in term time. They didn't take it well. I would definitely lose the bursary that paid half my fees if I was busted now, which amounted to the same thing as being kicked out anyway, I reflected, standing on the top step, wondering if it was too late to turn back.

"Psycho! Come on!" whispered Rupert. He was standing on the stairs in the darkness, turning back at me.

I liked the romance of being a rebel. My dad had been

a rebel when he was at Eton. One of the most important buildings in Eton was the imposing school library with an old cannon in the railed courtyard opposite it. My dad had told me that when he was at Eton he and a friend had filled up the cannon with bread rolls and blasted the library with them in the dead of night, using home-made dynamite that they had manufactured in the science schools. Another of his classic stories was about driving around the town with his rich friend who kept a Rolls-Royce at a garage in Eton. My dad would do an impression of how they would drive up and down the high street, his arms extended above his head, grasping the imaginary steering wheel. They hid beneath the dashboard whenever they saw an authority figure, using a mirror to view the road like submarine commanders.

Rupert shone the light in my face. "Come on!" he whispered again.

I went.

The cellar was very dusty and full of cobwebs. By the sweep of Rupert's torch I could see piles of old furniture and broken benches and chairs, familiar in design from the house assembly room. And there, in one corner, under a vaulted arch, and behind a locked metal grid, was the holy grail – Harrison's wine cellar.

The metal grid protecting the wine looked like it had been made several hundred years ago. It was medieval; big, wide strips of metal bolted together with screws. It was easy enough to reach your arm through, and, as Rupert had predicted, we were comfortably able to reach the outermost bottles. My heart was racing as I stretched my arm through the grid and slowly extracted one bottle after another. I took four in all, two for each of us.

Then we started back up the stairs. We held a bottle by the neck in each fist to stop them clinking. If we were caught now we were dead. But the house was dark and silent. We eased back the spring door and shut it behind us as quietly as we could, and tiptoed up the stairs. We hid the bottles in our rooms until the weekend, then snuck off to an island in the middle of the river which ran through the school to drink them.

It was the best wine I have ever tasted, before or since. And never mind the vintage. We didn't care about the quality. The point was we'd stuck it to the man.

Over the next few months I developed an unquenchable thirst for Dr Harrison's wine. Once, I even sold some of the bottles I had stolen to some other boys and just went back for more the next night. For the many months this went on it was like we had discovered a goose that laid golden eggs. But it had to come to an end. One night we got down there and discovered that someone – either he or a member of his staff – must have realised what was going on, and moved all the bottles to the back of the cellar, out of reach of our arms.

We were incensed, outraged, but we quickly came up with a plan. The next night I met Rupert in the bathroom and in addition to a torch he was also carrying a pop-out umbrella, a bamboo stick and a piece of string with a small lassoo at the end of it. We snuck down to Harrison's cellar for the last time, and by torch light began our most daring heist yet.

In silence, I used the bamboo stick to guide the flimsy lasso over the necks of the bottles beyond our reach. Then, I pulled the string tight with a few sharp jerks on the end of it, while Rupert pushed the folded umbrella through the grate. He pressed a button on the handle to extend it. It shot open with a tremendous amount of noise. Then he held the umbrella under the lassooed bottle and I gently pulled it out of the wine rack and it plopped into the umbrella. The umbrella held the weight, and we sighed with relief. We took six bottles of wine that night. We couldn't extricate the umbrella because we couldn't fold it up again to get it out of the grid, so we just left it there. As we sneaked up the stairs with our haul, I was thrilled by our ingenuity. I shone the flashlight back at the abandoned umbrella and suddenly understood why burglars like to take a crap in their victims' living rooms. There's really no better way to say "Fuck You".

I began to buy cannabis regularly. I would buy lumps of hashish from a Rastafarian who lived on the Portobello Road (at vastly inflated prices I later found out). I financed my habit easily using my father's occasional cheques.

Back at school, Rupert and I would sneak out of the house most nights to smoke dope in the subterranean, Second World War bomb shelter we had discovered at the bottom of my housemaster's garden. The happiest days of my school career were spent skinning up giant joints in that bomb shelter – which we dubbed The Nostril, because of its cylindrical shape. The Nostril was decorated with tatty drapes nailed or stuck to the concrete walls, and we sat in old chairs, sometimes as many as ten of us, a band of rene-gades on the lam from the bizarre world above. Down there I could drift away in a haze of sweet smoke, freed from all my worries by marijuana. I adored it. I spent hours there every night, listening to reggae on the crappy stereo and patching up wax leaks on the menhir-sized candles.

Above ground I was a failure, ashamed of my parents' brutal estrangement, ashamed that my father apparently didn't care about me, ashamed by my family's relative poverty and, to add insult to injury, I was useless at sport as well. But down here I was normal. Most of my friends who spent time in The Nostril hated and were hated by the school as much as I was. At last I could say I belonged to a group, a gang. This rebel stuff was something I could really be good at.

On my very last weekend at Eton, I went out drinking with Ben again. I furtively opened a bottle of wine under the railway arches with two girls we had met from a nearby boarding school. We drank one bottle, then invited them back to our house to drink some more.

I don't know what we were thinking of, why we didn't just go and drink the wine on the playing fields somewhere. But for some reason, we took them back to my room. We hadn't even got to the stage of getting their clothes off when we heard the sound of Dr Harrison charging around the house, flinging open doors, shouting, "SYKES!! WHITE!!"

All four of us looked one to the other in a panic.

"Quick! We've got to get you out of here," I shouted.

We ran down the corridor and bustled the girls out of the back entrance to the house. Then we heard Harrison yelling our names again. Ben and I split up, and ran to the top of the house up different staircases. Harrison followed me.

"SYKES! STOP!"

Just like that, I stopped, no longer a rebel, just another frightened and slightly drunk little boy. Harrison caught up with me and his face was bright red, shaking with rage. I looked out the window and saw the girls hurrying down the driveway.

He followed my gaze, then turned to me with a nasty expression on his face, his eyes burning over the tops of his half-moon glasses and said, "If those girls have been in the house, Sykes, you're for the long walk!"

He sprinted down the stairs at an impressive pace for a man in late middle age. Out of the window I watched him grab the girls and march them back to our house.

-5020 DAYS

a FEW DAYS LATER, my mother tearfully showed me a mealy-mouthed letter she had received from my housemaster. Dated March 20, 1991, and signed "David", it included my reports, "written mostly before disaster struck" and my GCSE certificates, which were "to be kept in a safe place" if I wanted "further education (or some jobs)".

Most bizarrely, the letter noted that I had out a copy of the French novel, *Manon Lescaut*, "which the school librarian would be glad to have back." I sat at the kitchen table gazing at Dr Harrison's concise, 150-word missive, staggered that he would think I would go to the trouble of posting back a book to the library of a school which had just expelled me. Needless to say, I never found the book anyway.

3

-5025 DAYS

i PACKED UP MY ROOM at Eton like a bad tenant skip-
ping out on the rent. I tore down a huge blue drape
from the wall and simply threw all my possessions into
it. Books, clothes, letters – everything went into the
drape. My friends all stood around the doorway to my
room, looking as horrified as they were thrilled by the
unfolding drama.

"What happened?" Rupert said.

What had happened was that the Head Man, Eric
Anderson, had rung our home – the rented cottage on my
uncle's estate – the night before and asked my mum to
come up to the school with me the next day. At that point
I had only been rusticated, albeit for a staggering three
weeks for the wine-and-girls-in-the-house episode. So we
had driven up to Eton the following day. I was fairly sure I
was about to be expelled – I knew this was the way it usually

happened – but Mum seemed blissfully unaware of my impending doom.

"I'm just going to tell Mr Anderton that he's *got* to let you stay," was all she would say when I suggested the meeting was likely to end with me getting the boot. We were whizzing round the motorway at about 90 mph and my mum was driving barefoot as usual.

"It's Anderson, Mum, not Anderton. Eric Anderson."

"Alright, Anderson. I mean, they've *got* to keep you. They *know* what we have been through as a family. They can't just wash their hands of you! Now, eat some of this flapjack. It's got sunflower seeds in it which will be really health-giving and good for your immune system."

I gazed listlessly out of the window at the familiar scenery flashing by.

"And, I mean, they can't just get rid of you after you were the star of that television programme," Mum said. I shuddered. A documentary had just been made about Eton life, and one scene – which pointed up how modern Eton's syllabus was – featured me murdering a few words of basic Japanese.

"Konichiwa!" I said to the camera.

In a supreme irony it had been shown just days ago. My poor mother had to endure dozens of phone calls from her friends congratulating her on *how well* I was doing despite the turmoil at home, while I sat as quietly as possible in another corner of the room.

"I mean…"

"Look out!" I screamed as we nearly rammed into the back of a lorry.

My mum didn't blink, dabbed the brakes and then hit the accelerator again, overtaking on the inside, turning her head ninety degrees to smile at me. I shut my eyes and gripped the handrest.

Mum's cars were always covered in dents. Usually I thought this was funny, I even took a perverse pride in them, evidence as they were of her indifference to bourgeois social conventions such as panel beating.

But when we pulled up outside the Head Man's office, a luxurious suite of rooms, each the size of a football pitch, housed in one of the school's oldest buildings, my mum's dented Nissan seemed just another embarrassing indictment, a reminder that people like us really had no business being at Eton in the first place.

I sat in one room adjacent to the Head Man's office while my mum went in to the other to see him. I sat there for half an hour. His secretary never looked up from her computer. I couldn't hear a word from inside the office. No sound from inside the office escaped the thick wool carpet or the solid oak doors.

Eventually she came out, shaking her head, and just saying, "No, no, it's no good, no good," over and again. She looked washed out.

I hugged her and said, "Mum, I'm so sorry."

Then we went to my house, neither of us in tears but both of us on the verge of them, where I went up to my room, shoved everything in that drape, told Rupert, "I got kicked out," grabbed the four corners of my giant bundle and half-pushed, half-carried the whole lot angrily down the stairs and forced it into the trunk of the car.

On the staircase wall, I noticed on the way down, somebody had already scratched, "TOM SYKES RIP". I climbed into the passenger seat and gritted my teeth.

We sped back round the motorway for the last time in a bubble of loaded silence. Eventually I coughed, and asked, "So what did he say?"

"He was *horrible*," my mum said, dabbing at her eyes now, the walls beginning to come down. "He just kept telling me over and over again that you needed to see a psychiatrist."

I didn't mention to Mum that I had actually been to see the school shrink at Eton. It hadn't gone well. I had burst into tears and sobbed, "My dad ... my dad ..." At the end of an hour the psychiatrist had said, "You're a very unhappy boy Tom. And I am afraid that I can't just wave a magic wand and make all this disappear." I made another appointment, but I never went back. What would have been the point?

My mum was still talking about the Head Man's treatment of her. "He was so cold. He just wanted me *out* of that office. He kept telling me, 'You must leave this office now, Mrs Sykes.' And I said 'No! Just talk to me Mr Anderton.' I wouldn't leave."

Oh my god, she had actually called him Anderton instead of Anderson. Good.

"He wouldn't even talk to me. He just wanted me *out*."

"Thanks Mum," I said. "I'm so sorry."

We lapsed into silence for another half hour.

"So what do you want to do?" my mother asked eventually, her voice quivering.

I had absolutely no idea what I wanted to do, but I thought I'd better say something. I was racked with guilt about what this latest disaster would do to her health. I wanted to be strong for her.

"I'll get a job," I said. "That way I can pay my way, be of use."

"How will you get a job?" asked my mother. It was a reasonable question. At sixteen I had a bunch of basic qualifications but still, I was hardly a killer hire.

I thought for a few seconds. "I'll go to the JobCentre. You can drop me off there on the way home."

An hour later she pulled into the car park at the JobCentre in the big town near our new house, Redhill.

"I'll get a train home," I said, as I got out of the car.

She drove off crying.

Christ. I felt awful. Despite her depression and illness, my mum had summoned all her last reserves of energy together to make the trip to Eton, to try to keep me in the school. Now that she had failed, it was as if she had sunk lower than ever. And it was all my fault. Or my dad's fault, depending how you looked at it.

When the car was out of sight, I walked over to a newsagent and bought a packet of cigarettes. I cupped a match smoothly in my hand to light one and smoked it thoughtfully, pacing around the pedestrianised town centre. I walked past a pub. I decided to duck in for a pint. Well, I could now, couldn't I? This was the whole point.

I sat at the bar in the smoky pub, thinking about my options. I had two: either I could get a job, or I could go back to school. Going back to school would be difficult – there was certainly no money to pay for me to go to a private school. The thought of going to a state school filled me with terror. I was pretty certain that I wouldn't survive more than a day or two outside the private system without being hospitalised.

But if I got a job, well, I would have money. I could go to pubs as much as I wanted. And I could smoke cigarettes and weed whenever the mood took me as well. Freedom – it sounded good. I thought of my dad and his never-ending resumé. Maybe I could go and work on an avocado farm in Tibet? Become a weapons dealer? I wondered if my Dad knew I had been expelled, then realised, *of course not, of course he doesn't*. No one had been in touch after all.

A guy in his twenties was sitting at the bar next to me. I ordered another pint and leaned across to him.

"Excuse me?" I asked in my cut-glass English.

"Yeah?" said the guy, in a strong West Country accent. He was wearing a chef's jacket and he had two yellowing front teeth and a day's worth of stubble on his face.

"Can I ask you a question? Do you have any academic qualifications?"

"No," said the bloke. He reacted to my question like I had just asked him if he was an axe murderer. "What's it to you?"

"Well, I've just been expelled from school and I was wondering whether I should get a job or go back to school."

He sighed, offered me one of his cigarettes, took a long draw of his and exhaled a blast of smoke in my direction. I took one and lit it.

"Right," he said. "I passed you in the street just a few minutes earlier and you nearly knocked me off my feet. Looked like you didn't know where you were going."

"Really? Sorry about that."

"Yeah, well, I could tell you looked a bit out of it. A bit spaced out."

Over our pints, I told him the whole story.

He nodded sympathetically every three seconds until I got to the end. I offered to buy him a pint.

"Yeah. Right. Lovely. Stella please."

We were getting on like a house on fire now. Maybe it was not the case that anyone without a posh accent would want to kick my head in after all.

"OK," I said, ordering the drinks. "So what would you do?"

"Well," he said slowly, pondering his pronouncement prophetically. "I'd say fuck it and have a laugh. Doesn't sound to me like you want to go back to that Eton place anyway. I mean, it's good about the pub there and all, but it sounds like its full of fucking faggots to me. Go and get a job! I started working when I was sixteen, and, you know, at least that way you've always got a few quid in your pocket. You know, get some girls and that."

I thanked him, finished my pint and walked over to the JobCentre. I took a ticket and waited in line to see an employment adviser.

The employment adviser turned out to be a bored, thirty-year-old woman who kept filing her nails throughout our brief interview. Every opportunity she got she would make a tutting noise and roll her eyes to indicate that I was wasting her time and she was way above all this anyway.

"I need a job," I told her. Tut. Eye roll.

"I have ten GCSEs." Silence.

Eventually, she spoke. "Ever worked before?" she asked.

"No," I said. She sighed heavily, rummaged around her desk for a few moments and then pulled out a job card.

"Strawberries," she said, pushing the card over to me.

I looked at the card. It was an opportunity to join a fast-growing fruit wholesaling firm, working as a key provider of raw product to the distribution chain.

It took a moment for the penny to drop. "You want me to pick strawberries?" I asked. "But, I've got ten GCSEs in English, Maths, Science, Latin… Is there nothing else available? Something in an office?"

"Can you type?" she asked with a sigh.

"No," I said.

"Then it's strawberries," she said. "Take it or leave it." She exhaled dramatically and looked at her watch.

It paid £7 per hour. I took it.

-5024 DAYS

STRAWBERRIES are the summer totem of the English moneyed classes. The newspapers report breathlessly how many tons of them will be devoured at sporting events like Wimbledon and Henley, overpriced and served in little foam bowls with a dollop of cream and a sprinkling of sugar. They are piled gleefully into huge pyramids at weddings as signifiers of good fortune, harbingers of financial security.

But at 7am the morning after my interview at the job centre, as I stood in the middle of a vast strawberry field, plants stretching as far as the eye could see, wondering what the fuck had happened to my life, I hated strawberries. They mocked me.

Ten days ago I had been wearing a tail suit studying Shakespeare. Now, clad in a pair of old jeans and a dispensable white T-shirt, I couldn't help feeling a little sorry for myself as I bent over, and began working my way down the line of plants, one foot planted on either side of the row.

I had been picking for about thirty minutes when the supervisor came past me and inspected my basket. He was a middle-aged man with a bushy black moustache and even in the open air he stank of fermenting fruit.

"What the fuck do you call this then?" he said, nudging my basket with the tip of his Wellington boot.

"Er, well," I started, but he cut me off.

"A bloody waste of money, that's what it is!" he bellowed at me.

All around in the giant field, with the pale early morning sun rising in the east, the other workers were standing up, hands on their hips, taking a break to watch the entertainment.

"Look at these, they are all mush!" he said picking up one of the strawberries in my basket. It was falling apart because I hadn't picked it properly. I had left the stalk behind on the plant. "I can't sell that. That's no good for nothing but ... jam. You'd better pick your game up sonny or you'll be out on your arse."

"Sorry," I muttered as he wandered on down the line, "I'm new."

He turned back and yelled, "I don't care if you're the King of England. If you can't pick a sodding strawberry you're no good to me."

About 11am we had a break. I drank a can of Coke as all the workers congregated on a patch of grass between the strawberry fields and the raspberry plants we were about to move on to. I sucked my fingers, stained red with strawberry juice.

A tough-looking guy with a shaved head and tattoos on his knuckles walked up to me. "So what you doing here?" he asked. I was transfixed as he professionally rolled up and lit a cigarette in a fraction of a second.

"I just got expelled from school," I said, trying to roughen up my accent a little. "What about you?"

"Just got out," he said.

"Oh. Out of where?" I asked. He looked in his mid thirties.

He paused for a long moment, drew his chin down to his neck and frowned at me. "Prison," he said, disdainfully.

"Oh, right," I said, as casually as I could, as if I hung out with ex-prisoners every day of the week. "What were you in for?"

He looked at me for an even longer moment. "Manslaughter," he said. Then he stuck out his hand, "I'm Tony."

-5010 DAYS

ONY TURNED OUT to be a pretty good guy. At the end of my second week, when I got my first pay packet, Tony gave me a lift to the pub. He threw my bicycle that I used to get to and from the farm in the back of his beaten-up old truck, and drove violently at knuckle-whitening speed to a rough pub a few miles away. Because we started work so early, we were finished by 2.30pm, drinking our first pints in the beer garden – a grand name for what was actually a patch of roughly paved outside space. A main road roared by noisily a few yards behind us, hidden by a stained black fence. The garden smelt of the steam from the dishwasher we could hear clanking away in the kitchen, which jutted out of the main building.

We bitched about the strawberry farm and the supervisor for a little bit, then the conversation inexorably turned to our past lives.

"So you just got expelled from school right?" he asked. Flush with his pay packet, Tony was smoking normal cigarettes instead of roll-ups today. "Straights" he called them.

"Yeah," I said, and I told him some stories about Eton. When I finished, he laughed and said, "Well, first time I ever had a pint with an old Etonian."

"First time I ever had a pint with a manslaughterer," I chanced, emboldened by the beer, and we both laughed, tipping our heads back to feel the sun.

Tony didn't get into the details about his crime but he was happy to tell me about the prisons where he been "banged up". We sat in the garden and drank pint after pint that sunny afternoon, as Tony told me how he made alcohol in his cell by fermenting oranges underneath his bed.

"I was fucking good at making orange wine," he kept repeating. "I was famous for it. I never went short. Cigarettes, porn, dope, I could always trade my wine for whatever I wanted. I was famous for it. I was fucking good at making orange wine..."

Somewhere around the sixth pint I became aware that Tony was stuck in an alcoholic loop, repeating himself over and over again. It freaked me out a little bit because I had drunk the same amount as him. I went into the pub to take a piss.

It was pitch black inside after the bright light outside. I stumbled down some steps and the bar woman looked up sharply from her newspaper behind the bar.

"You all right?" she asked, her tone accusatory, not concerned. I was transfixed by her cigarette smoke coiling up from the ashtray on the bar, ethereal in the beams of sunlight that came in through the leaded windows.

"Yes," I said and stumbled blindly towards the bathroom.

In the bathroom I had a piss, then leaned against the wall over the sink, my hands either side of the mirror. I touched my forehead to the glass and grinned at my reflection. I thought of all my old friends at Eton. I checked my watch. They would just be finishing lessons about now. I pitied them their long weekend, trying to dodge the school authorities to get drunk.

This was life. What would I rather be doing – homework, or swapping stories with a bona fide killer over a packet of cigarettes and six pints of Stella? I looked at myself in the mirror and said, "You're free. You're free."

I spent the weekend quietly at home. The following Monday as I picked up my collecting basket at the strawberry farm I looked around for Tony. He was nowhere to be seen. All the rest of the week, he didn't show up. I finally saw him on the Friday, when he turned up to get his pay for the previous week.

"Fuck this for a laugh," he said, as he collected his money in a brown paper envelope. "I've got better things to do with my life than pick fucking strawberries. Wanna go to the pub?"

Sure. I always wanted to go to the pub.

-4996 DAYS

TWO WEEKS LATER I was fired from the strawberry farm for taking a pot of cream to work with me and sitting down in my break and eating the produce.

"What do you think this is?" the fermented-fruit smelling supervisor yelled when he saw me, reclining on the mud between the furrows, a juicy, cream-coated strawberry on its way to my lips. "Fucking Wimbledon?"

That afternoon I sat in the bath tub at home for over an hour, trying to get the red off my fingers and considering my options afresh.

My back ached from crouching over all day every day. I was exhausted. I had saved a grand total of £150. I was only sixteen, but still, I realised a hundred and fifty quid wasn't going to get me very far. Maybe the chef I had spoken to was wrong. Maybe this work stuff wasn't all it was cracked up to be.

I was thinking the unthinkable; maybe I should go back to school?

4

-4976 DAYS

ONE OF THE SMARTEST things I ever did after I got fired from the strawberry farm was make an appointment to go and see the headmaster at my local school and beg to be allowed to enrol there, even though by now it was well over halfway through the academic year, just a few days before the summer term was due to begin.

Initially the headmaster, Roger Coles, a bearded man in his fifties, insisted that I would have to repeat a year because the syllabuses at Eton and Oxted were not the same.

I told him that if I had to wait I probably wouldn't go back to school. He looked at the history teacher, Mr Pickford, who was sitting in on our interview in Mr Coles's small file-cluttered office, which was roughly one-tenth the size of Eric Anderson's. Mr Pickford, the head of history, which was one of my subjects, had a giant nose and wild curly hair that was so long and bushy it was on the point of becoming an Afro.

"Well, he's probably done more than most of our kids," said Mr Pickford with a heavy nasal twang. "So I say, come on down."

"All right then," said Mr Coles. He pushed a scrap of photocopied paper towards me, which had the dates of the new term written on it. At Eton, the term dates were all contained in a smartly bound green notebook with Fixtures written on the front.

"Monday 15 April," I read out loud. "Thank you so much. I'll see you then."

"Oh no, no," said Mr Coles. "Actually that's wrong. Term actually starts on the Tuesday."

"Oh, OK," I said, a little confused. I looked from him to Mr Pickford. "See you on Tuesday then."

It wasn't till a couple of years later that I found out that term had indeed started on the Monday, as it said on the photocopy. But Mr Coles hadn't wanted me there on the Monday. Because on the Monday, the first day of term, he had gone into morning assembly and given the school a pep talk, using me as its basis.

He stood up, in front of the whole school, and said, "This is the best state school in the whole of Surrey! And do you know how I know that? Because tomorrow, we've got an Old Etonian joining us!" He didn't, of course, mention that I had been expelled from Eton in disgrace.

Meanwhile I was at home, working out what I was going to wear, and perfecting my new, tougher accent that I had been working on over the last few weeks.

I was terrified that I was going to be beaten to a pulp. One of my only friends who didn't go to Eton was a guy called Tom Freud. Our parents had been friends. Tom lived in London and went to a tough state school.

I phoned him to ask his advice. How should I handle myself?

"Well," he said thoughtfully, "I think the mistake new kids make is that they try and be part of the gang right away. Like we have this game, when we are eating our lunch, to all try and push each other off this step. And this new guy turned up last term and right away he was trying to push us off the step. He was too quick to try and jump in. You know, you've got to play it cool. You'll be fine, Tommy."

Don't push anyone off a step, I thought to myself as I cycled to school the next day. *Play it cool and you'll be fine.*

Around 2,500 students attended Oxted County School, the same number as Eton, but that was where the similarities ended. Instead of being spread out over a town, with schoolrooms housed in centuries-old buildings, Oxted County conducted its pedagogy in several modern structures squeezed into a couple of cramped acres on the edge of the town. When the bell rang at the end of lessons there were human traffic jams in the playgrounds as the kids tried to get to their next class. Famous old boys at Eton included Percy Bysshe Shelley and Pitt the Younger. At Oxted, as far as I was aware, our most notable alumnus was one of the great train robbers. It wasn't even Ronnie Biggs – just one of his lesser-known accomplices.

At 2pm I had my first free period, and I followed a crowd of kids out of the school gates to have a cigarette round the corner. I couldn't quite believe no one stopped me. I stood a little way apart from them and lit up, half wishing I had the courage to go over and introduce myself, and half thinking that I needed to play it cool. *Don't push anyone off the step.*

A big green car pulled up next to me and an enormous teenager heaved his massive frame out of the passenger seat of the car. *This is it*, I thought to myself, *I'm going to be beaten to a pulp.*

"Got a fag?" the giant asked me. He had a low boom-ing voice.

"Sure," I said, flipping open my box, working on my new, tougher accent.

"Thanks," he said, accepting a light. "Are you new then?"

"Yeah," I said, desperately trying to speak as little as possible so as not to give the game away. "You?"

"I left," he said. "My name's Neil." Neil was about 6ft 3in and his voice was deep, loud and slow.

"I'm Tom," I said.

Another guy had got out of the car and came to join us. "I'm Robin," he said, as he messed around with a rolling paper and a pouch of loose tobacco. He had blond curly hair, and didn't say much.

We stood smoking in the sun for a little bit. "Well, this is fucking boring," said Neil, after a while, and he turned to Robin. "Want to go up to the J-Tree?"

"Sure," said Robin. "I've got a little bit of hash."

"Want to come up to the woods with us?" asked Neil.

"Sure," I said, as nonchalantly as I could. Were we really about to get into the car and drive off to the woods for a joint while school was still going on? Apparently so. Maybe Oxted County school was going to be okay after all.

Robin's car was an old green Vauxhall Viva, and as we drove up into the woods above Oxted he rolled another cigarette with his right hand, steered with his knees and shifted the gearstick with his left.

"Ooops," he would say every time the car lurched toward the verge.

This seemed to annoy Neil. "Robin can you just keep your bloody hands on the wheel please. Here, have one of my cigarettes rather than one of those roll-ups."

Robin took one and slyly smiled.

We made it to the woods, and parked up under a giant oak tree anchored into the ground with massive, knotted roots, its branches spreading out above us, filtering the afternoon sunshine.

"I'll skin up," said Robin, producing a little block of hash from somewhere inside the car. He began burning it with his lighter and crumbling it into some rolling papers. He pulled out his bag of tobacco and was about to add some when Neil said, in an exasperated tone that suggested they had had this conversation before, "Please don't use that disgusting tobacco, Robin. Here, have one of my cigarettes."

I thought I saw Robin do his sly smile again as he reached out for the cigarette without looking up from the papers. These guys could push each other's buttons like an old married couple. Robin licked the cigarette down the seam and pulled it open halfway, spreading the tobacco onto the hash. He rolled up the joint and we smoked it sitting on the bonnet of the car, while Robin played a Pat Metheny album on the stereo.

"Please," said Neil. "Can you turn this terrible music off?"

"No," said Robin. "It's my car and the man's a genius."

So I sat there and listened to Pat Metheny in the woods with my new friends Robin and Neil. They asked me what I was doing at the school and I thought, well, what the hell, we're stoned, we're together, we're friends now, and I told them about Eton.

"Oh right," said Robin. "You're Tom *Sykes*."

"Yeah?" I said.

"You live next door to my grandma. She told me about you."

Robin's grandma, Molly Delwiche, lived in a tiny, immaculate, Victorian terraced house at the bottom of the driveway of the house owned by my uncle in which we were living. After that, when Robin came to visit his grandmother he would come up and knock on my door. He was supposed to be at school but he wasn't there much. He and the school had both lost interest in each other. At Oxted there were few serious attempts to get truants into school if, like Robin, they were over sixteen, the legal school-leaving age. With thirty kids or so in each class – compared to eight or nine at

Eton – the teachers had enough on their plate without chasing down missing students.

Robin's dad was an electrician and his mum was a nurse, and they lived just a few miles away from me in Godstone. For lots of reasons Robin became one of my closest friends at Oxted. There was the geographical proximity of his grandma to my house, there was the fact that it wasn't too far out of his way to pick me up on the way to the pub on Friday and Saturday nights, and there was the fact we both liked smoking pot. After the pub we would lumber around the country lanes in his massive, gas-guzzling motor and park in out-of-the-way lanes to smoke hash and listen to Robin's eclectic music collection. He was into rare jazz, Frank Zappa and Funkadelic. These days he is a recording engineer.

One summer Saturday night we drove into the countryside after the pub as usual. We parked in the entrance to a field by a locked gate. We were smoking a joint when a police car pulled up behind us and flashed its lights twice.

"Oh shit," we both said simultaneously. We tried to grab the dope and the papers but a young cop was already banging on the window with a flashlight. They found the marijuana, of course, and hauled us down to the police station. There, they split us up, and strip-searched me. I had to take off all my clothes while I was standing on a plastic sheet. Then the officer told me to squat down.

"Why?" I asked, "Do you think I have drugs wedged in my butt cheeks?"

"Just squat please, Mr Sykes," he said, in a tone that

suggested this was more painful for him than it was for me.

After that they led me to a cell. The cell was just a square room built of unpainted cinder blocks, with a metal toilet, a wooden bench built into the wall and a door with a viewing window.

I sat down on the bench. This was the second time I had been in a police cell in my life; the first time was the incident two years previously when I had been caught riding my sister's moped. I felt much less concerned this time round. The law had been gradually shifting towards the decriminalisation of cannabis over the past few years, and considering the tiny amount of resin we had on us – less than an eighth of an ounce – we were unlikely to get anything more than a caution. They probably wouldn't even call my mum. Still it wasn't exactly a great place to be.

I lay back on my bench, with my hands behind my head, and started reading the graffiti. I was only mildly surprised to recognise some of the names of kids who went to my school. One tag, written over a smiley face, read, "Smiffy woz 'ere!"

After a few hours, the same young policeman came and opened my cell door. I followed him down the passageway to a door marked Interview Room.

The room was painted an unsettling shade of green. He took my fingerprints and then sat me down, at which point another, older, more senior officer came into the room.

He began by asking me a few perfunctory questions, then he leaned across the table and switched the tape recorder off with a dramatic flourish.

"So," the cop said, puffing up his red cheeks. "Where did you get the stuff? Tell us where you got it and you're out of here, no record."

I was still high and I tried not to laugh. This guy was playing the part of a cop he had seen on some TV show. They had found less than ten quids-worth of hash on me. I wasn't exactly looking at jail time.

"Think it's funny, eh?" he said. "Well, let me tell you something. Your friend Robin is over the legal blood-alcohol limit and unless you tell us where you got this stuff, we're going to do him for drunk driving."

Now this was serious. If Bobby couldn't drive how would I get to the pub? I had to do it. I gave them the name. "We got it from a guy called Greg," I said.

He nodded. "Greg. Right. Thanks very much. Surname, please."

"I can't give you his surname," I protested.

"Give it to me or your friend Robin gets a breath test," he replied.

I sighed. "Greg Davidson," I said, telling them the truth. "He lives in Redhill."

The policeman gave a badly hidden I-told-you-so-smile to his junior. "Great. That's it. You can go now Mr Sykes."

I stood up and followed the young cop out of the cell and down the corridor to the front of the station. Robin was waiting for me there. We looked at each other sheepishly.

The young policeman actually drove us back to Robin's car, although he clearly knew he was over the limit. "Mind how you go now," he said as he dropped us off.

The car was unlocked. We got in and sat there in silence for a few moments.

"I can't believe they didn't breath test me," said Robin eventually.

"They said they would unless I told them who we got the dope off," I said. The headlights from a passing car washed over Robin's face. On this little lane it was probably the policeman heading back to the station, but I couldn't tell.

"Me too," said Robin. We sat in silence for a moment then both said simultaneously, "I told them it was Greg."

We looked at each other and then cracked up laughing.

"Well, you know, sod it," I said. "It's true. Why should you lose your licence? The guy makes enough money. Occupational hazard."

We knew we had broken the code by grassing Greg up though, and as Bobby drove me home we justified what we had done.

"He lives in Redhill…"

"He's small time, they won't go after him…"

"That copper was just playing tough…"

Eventually Robin said, "And I only gave them his first name. I mean, there must be loads of people called Greg dealing pot round here."

I went silent for a bit. Then I said, "I gave them the last name too."

Another silence. Then I said, "Ooops."

We thought for a beat. "Well, he's fucked then," Robin said, and we both collapsed into stoned giggles again.

5

-4553 DAYS

URING THE SUMMER of 1992, the year after I was
expelled from Eton, things started to really improve
at home for the first time since my dad left. We moved out
of my uncle's house and my mum bought her own house in
Oxted. It was on the side of a major road, next door to one
of Oxted's roughest pubs, the Wheatsheaf, and very oddly
designed. When you walked in the front door off the street,
you were confronted with two impossibly steep staircases –
one going up to two bedrooms and one going down to the
kitchen, sitting room and garden. It was much, much smaller
than the cottage my uncle had lent us, which I now realised
was not a cottage at all but a substantial country residence.

One thing that our new house did have going for it was
that by a strange quirk, the garden ran into about two acres
of woodland that was technically owned by the local council
but was effectively part of our garden. It had a little river

running through it, and my uncle had allowed me to disassemble an old chicken shed that was in the garden of the cottage and take it to Riverside -- as our new house was called.

The reason my uncle had let me take the shed with us was because I had kitted it out with armchairs, sofas and a stereo. When the shed relocated with us to Oxted my popularity exploded. The new house, as well as being next door to the Wheatsheaf, was just down the road from the Crown, the pub we all used to drink in.

The heart and soul of the shed crew was me, Robin, Neil, Simon, a computer whizz-kid, and Steve, a budding hippy with a ponytail. We kitted it out with armchairs, hooked up an extension cord all the way up the garden to the house and put a barbecue outside.

We would meet there most nights to get stoned. My mother did not turn a blind eye to the pot so much as she just never saw it. She didn't know what to look for. She hardly ever drank and had never taken drugs – alcohol makes her feel sick. Poachers make the best gamekeepers, but my mum was blissfully ignorant.

Mentally, Mum was now much better than when my dad had left. She had thrown away all her anti-depressants and her new drug of choice seemed to be painting the crazy staircase different colours. At least once a fortnight, during the painting mania, I would come home, put the key in the front door and find it was bolted. So I would have to walk round the back way, climb over the fence to the shed and walk up the garden, to find my mum, paintbrush in hand, brewing incredibly strong coffee and painting the hallway and stairs silver, lavender or green.

Every month or so, however, terrible migraines would strike her down for five or six days on end. Fred, who was nine now, and Josh, who was four, would tip-toe silently around the house filled with foreboding. I would cook eggs for them, trying to be the responsible adult. Sometimes I would invite them down to the shed in the evenings where they would join in with my mates and cook sausages over the fire on the sharpened ends of sticks. They were too small to ask too many questions about the "funny cigarettes" we made.

So my mum wasn't really doing the teenage drug-watch thing. "I was just happy you were making friends after you were expelled from that awful school," she told me, years later, when I asked her about it. "I thought it was lovely that everyone would come round and see you. I really had no idea about the drugs. And I thought the drinking and being sick was, well, just pure *naughtiness*. It's what boys do."

My friends loved coming to my house. Mum, who has always had her hair stained bright red with henna, would make us coffee and flapjacks when we got the munchies. Fred would carry them down to the shed on a tray. She was always trying to make my friends eat yogurt and pumpkin seeds. Her personal health strategy still revolves around the production and consumption of vast amounts of home-made yogurt. Her belief in it as a universal panacea is so powerful she can't let someone step through the door without forcefully offering them a bowlful.

In the shed, we were pursuing our own route to enlightenment with the aid of LSD. We bought tabs for a few pounds each, and then we would wander around Oxted tripping our heads off for several hours before heading back to the shed to listen to music and smoke pot – which we still sometimes bought from Greg, the guy I had grassed up, but who, to my great relief, never got busted.

I loved acid but the intensity of the experience always scared me as well. My visions would morph dangerously towards the nightmarish if I shut my eyes for too long. I seemed to spend most of my time waiting to come down. Steve and Neil took a trip and had communal visions that the trees were getting up and walking around on their roots, chasing them, coming to get them. Neil quit all drugs as a result. Steve was not so easily put off.

Their bad trip scared me, but I reassured myself that they had made mistakes. They had taken too many trips, mixed halves and quarters of different batches, asked for trouble.

Still, I never kidded my self that acid was safe, and my bad trip came at Glastonbury. The festival took place right after the end of term, and I was on a bender to celebrate the fact that I had finished school. I had sworn off drugs and alcohol for two months before my A-levels and I suspected I would do well enough, when the results came through, to get into my first-choice university, Edinburgh.

So Glastonbury was a real party. It was gorgeous weather. We had been tripping all day, wandering around the festival laughing hysterically at the various sideshow freaks. I sat down to have a cup of coffee with Steve, several hours after the trip had worn off. With no warning at all I went into convulsions.

Suddenly I was seven feet above the ground looking down on myself. My head was thrown way back, and I could only see the whites of my eyes. I looked like I was having a fit.

From my vantage point up in the sky, I could see all around. My mind was very clear. I was dying, there was absolutely no doubt about it. I rose up, higher and higher in the sky, ten feet, twenty feet, maybe more. My head remained the centre of my vision. I could see the paper coffee cup on the table, even the coffee stand where I had bought my coffee. Thousands of festival-goers were milling around me. To my left sat my friend Steve. He had grabbed my arm and he was shaking me, shouting something I couldn't hear. I was up there for several seconds before I noticed that the other guy sitting at our table was this boy, Matthew Mole, who I didn't actually like that much. He'd been following our group around for about a year now.

"In fact," I thought, outraged, "He's a pain in the arse that guy." There was no way I was going to die with Matthew Mole sitting next to me. He'd be dining out on this anecdote for years.

I was panicking. I had to get out of this. I tried to dive down, and suddenly I was plummeting, and then I was back, back in my body again. My eyes rolled forward in their sockets and I could hear what Steve was screaming, "FUCK TOM FUCK FUCK FUCK."

I looked at him, swiveled my head a few degrees to the right and shot a stream of projectile out of my stomach.

I'll never forget the extraordinary sound of a hundred-plus people simultaneously shouting, "URRGGH" as the puke either hit them or flew past their faces.

Steve was screaming, "TOM TOM ARE YOU ALL RIGHT? ANSWER ME ARE YOU ALL RIGHT?"

I was. I felt 1000% sober. I looked at him with wide eyes. "I'm fine man," I said. "You won't believe what just happened to me."

I never took acid again.

-4222 DAYS

INSTEAD I SWITCHED to ecstasy. Ecstasy was sweeping the nation when I began taking it in 1992. It cost £25 a pop, and the pills were huge, purple lozenges – horse pills we used to joke.

We would go to the rave clubs in the East End of London. One night six of us piled into two cars and we headed up to Club UK with pills hidden in our shoes and our underwear to get past the bouncers. As soon as we got inside we popped the little tablets, washing them down with a shared bottle of water. The first thirty minutes were spent, as usual, trying to work out whether or not the pills we had bought were duds.

"Are you feeling anything yet?" Steve, Robin, Simon and I asked each other incessantly, as we wandered around the club. Club UK was an enormous venue which could accommodate two thousand revellers in four or five different rooms. Each room played a different kind of music.

Then, suddenly, a warm feeling started tingling in my stomach, followed swiftly by an overwhelming urge to take a crap. I knew from experience that this was not an impulse that should, on any account, be acted on.

Then the beat kicked in, the bass pumping through my thorax, reverberating in my chest and I wanted to dance. I didn't care anymore where Steve or Robin were. I didn't care who was watching. I couldn't help it – my hands were in the air, there is a stupid grin on my face. The lights start moving faster and faster and suddenly I get it, and the whole club, the whole *world* actually, is dancing along with me.

As I pump the air manically with my arms – a shy public schoolboy no more – I realise that I feel happy, happier than I have ever felt before in my life. Sweaty football hooligans with shaved heads come up to me and say "I love you man!" and we hug and laugh. Girls, pretty girls, beautiful girls with deep, dark eyes and skin shining with sweat are dancing with me. Then I'm kissing them, and they are kissing me, slimy and gorgeous and damp, the texture of tongue, and we are all dancing together, laughing, laughing, laughing.

As the pills wore off and the club emptied out, I headed

for the exit. The lads were all standing around outside. We go back to the cars and drove home, smoking a joint and talking about the night, listening to more tunes on a pirate radio station.

Just as we went through Streatham, with the sun coming up, a giant flock of pigeons, there must have been hundreds of them, darkened the sky. They came fast and low down the street, swooping back on themselves, drowning out the radio with their cries.

"Woaah!!" we all yelled together. "What was that?"

For a little while we drove on in silence, except for the breakbeats on the radio.

Back at my house, down at the shed, we drank tea, and smoked some more joints, stretching like big cats in the early morning sunshine, amazed and awed and over-whelmed at what ecstasy had given us.

6

-4090 DAYS

EDINBURGH was just like me – it was either getting drunk or in the throws of a ruinous hangover. Most people choose their university on the basis of where they are likely to get the best education in their chosen subject, along with other considerations such as where their friends are going or the cost of living. My major consideration in choosing Edinburgh University was Scottish licensing laws. In Edinburgh the pubs were open late.

There was a famous pub called the Phoenix just round the corner from where I lived on Broughton Street. It was open till 2am and reopened at 6am as an "early morning house". The official line was that this was so postal workers could have a few pints after they came off the night shift. The reality, at 6am, was a bar six-deep with students, clubbers and alcoholics fighting for a drink to keep their buzz on from the night before. Oasis and Blur blared out of the jukebox and marijuana smoke billowed out of the booths. I went back to visit a few years after I had left university and asked John the landlord if they were still open at 6am. "Och no," he said shaking his head. "It just got too feckin' busy. We dinnae open 'til eight now."

The Phoenix was a magical place for me and my friends. It wasn't run down in the slightest, but it was simple, straightforward and unpretentious. The floor was covered in brown carpets, the booths were brown leather and the room was dominated by an enormous oak bar. They sold pints for £1.50 and toasted sandwiches for 90 pence. So I ate there, I drank there, I cashed my cheques there. I even took my future wife there on our first date.

I met Sasha on Valentine's Day 1997. I was twenty-two, in my last year at university and we were both taking part in a blind date game organised by some friends of mine every year for singletons on Valentine's Day. I had seen Sasha a few times before when I had been delivering hash to a friend of hers, and I got my friends to rig the dating lottery so I could take Sasha out. I was told to meet her at the corner of Broughton Street. So that we could recognise each other, I was told to smoke a cigar while she would be drinking a can of lager.

About twenty minutes later I spied Sasha walking up Broughton Street. The first thing I noticed about her was that she was shorter than me, about 5ft 7in, had long blonde hair, and massive boobs. She was wearing flared jeans, and carrying a strappy bag over her shoulder. Her can of lager was empty. I tossed my cigar and leapt over the fence to greet her and kissed her hello. Then I took her to the Phoenix for a drink. Who said chivalry is dead?

Sasha sat on a leather bench and I sat on a stool, with a view of the bar, which meant I could just flick my hand at the bartender and he would bring another two pints over. Sasha is Irish, so we drank Guinness. The barman ran me a tab, and we quickly lost count of how much we drank. I deliberately set out to get her as drunk as possible so I could get her to come home with me. Things went well.

Sasha was studying to be an architect, and I wanted to be a writer and we seemed to connect on every level. I was fascinated by her Irishness, it seemed rare and exotic to me, and she was intrigued by my story of being expelled from Eton. Before we knew, it was 2am, and the pub was closing. We walked along the street, amorous from the Guinness, heading back to my house.

Much later that night, Sasha was in my bedroom. I peeled off her clothes while she lay in my bed. Her skin was pale white. Her boobs were every bit as fabulous as her clothed figure suggested. Just as I started to get my own clothes off she suddenly yelped, grabbed the duvet and ran out of my room. I was puzzled, and drunkenly surrendered to sleep.

When I woke up, she was gone, and I had no idea what had happened. A few days later when I rang and asked her to go out with me again she said yes. I was delighted. Finally

I had found a girl who could drink as much as me. This had to be the perfect woman.

My best friend at university was Olly Taylor. We lived together for the whole four years of college, spending the last two years in a huge tenement flat with 18-foot-high ceilings and wood floors on Leith Walk that was owned by my friend Nick. It was perfect because it was just around the corner from the Phoenix and we only had to pay £50 a week in rent.

University was supposed to shape our minds, but many of us set about assiduously frying ours instead. Most nights Olly, Nick and me would head out to the pub at about 10pm, and drink until 1 or 2 in the morning. Then, back home, Olly and I would listen to some music, I would skin up and finally we would crash out about 3. I would wake at 10 or 11am, except on Fridays when I had a 9am tutorial.

A few of my close friends actually lost their minds altogether. One stopped smoking marijuana in the last year at Edinburgh because it gave him such severe panic attacks. Another friend did so much acid that he had to be sectioned in an asylum after breaking into the landlady's bedroom in a pub and getting into her bed.

In our first year Olly and I shared an apartment with two other girls. One of them got pregnant but didn't tell anyone. When she had the baby, in secret, it died, and she hid the body in the freezer of her flat in London. We only found out what had happened when swarms of newspaper reporters descended on the university offering anyone who knew her tens of thousands of pounds for photographs of her with her boyfriend. The only heartwarming thing about the whole saga was that everyone told the reporters to get lost.

I walked around in a daze for weeks afterwards wondering how such a thing could have happened under my nose. Had she been pregnant when we were living with her? Why hadn't she asked us for help? Surely it didn't have anything to do with the joints, the Es and the three bottles of wine we shared every night?

The drug- and alcohol-fuelled insanity at Edinburgh made me feel sane, normal, boring even. All I did was drink a lot, smoke a lot of pot, and take speed or ecstasy at the weekend (I could only afford cocaine very occasionally). *I* was fine. *I* had never been sectioned. *I* didn't have any bodies in the ice compartment. It was *fun*.

But still, I was aware something was happening. When I went to Edinburgh I was a social drinker – a heavy one, given to frequent binges, but definitely a social drinker. I could go a few days without alcohol, and when I wanted to stop I would go home to bed. But somehow, by the time I left, I had lost control. I would wake up in the mornings suffering memory loss, wondering what I had done the night before, nervous about finding out the answer, ashamed. Somewhere during those four years of indulgence I stepped off the ledge and into the deep water. I spent a lot of time later in my life trying to work out just where that point was.

It might have been when my sister Plum called me, and told me she was worried about me. She'd heard tales about my drinking, even though she was living several thousand miles away in New York by then, where she had been hired by American *Vogue*. I agreed with her that I should quit drinking for six months. I was dry for about six hours.

Maybe I scrambled the eggs when my tutor who I saw every Friday at 9am asked me to stay behind at the end of class. When it was just us left in the room, he shut the door and asked me whether I had a problem with drinking as I had never showed up to his class on time and/or not smelling of booze.

"No, no," I said. "It's just the class starts so early."

"Nine am is not early, Tom," he said. "Unless you've been out till three in the morning the night before."

I left his class determined to *do something* about my problem. What I *did* was to circle around the student health centre, toying with the idea of going in and saying, *"I'm an addict,"* then think *I'm fine*, walk home, skin up a giant joint, put on a Funkadelic CD and get into bed for the rest of the day.

Or maybe the moment I broke the tape was when I ran to the bathroom at the Phoenix, threw up and came back to the bar and ordered another pint.

In the end, of course, it doesn't really matter when I became an alcoholic. One moment I reached down and the sand was there and the next time I tried, I couldn't touch the bottom anymore. Once you are in the deep water, the current gets stronger faster. It sucks you further and further out, out to a place where you can't really see the land and the people walking around on the beach building sandcastles anymore. All you see are other people who have been caught by the tide. Some of the people are even further out than you. And you say to yourself, *Well, I could swim back any time I like. But maybe I'll give it another hour or so. It's fun out here. The beach looks kind of boring anyway.*

7

-2624 DAYS

I DIDN'T QUIT DRINKING for my final exams at Edinburgh but I did stop smoking pot for three months. The transformation was quite incredible. I could remember things. I could focus for more than twenty minutes at a time. I only had to read a paragraph once to make sense of it. I crammed four years' worth of work into those twelve weeks. After I took my last exam I celebrated by buying an ounce bag of grass from my dealer James.

I moved down to London, where I rented a disgusting apartment with my friends Olly and Tom Craig above a kebab shop. I managed to get an appointment to see Stephen Clackson, the news editor of the London *Evening Standard*. We met in the work cafeteria, which was located in the vast glass-covered atrium of Associated Newspapers, just off Kensington High Street, where Clackson chain-smoked Gauloises cigarettes while I showed him my cuttings book. It had about ten pieces I had written for various university publications carefully glued into it. He started leafing through them, when his mobile phone went off and he had to run back to his desk.

"Look, I've got to go," he said, scooping my cuttings book under his arm, "But I'll take a look at these later."

"Oh," I said, freaking out because he was about to disappear with my only asset in my quest for a job in journalism. "Couldn't I copy them for you or something?"

He paused, looked at me sternly, and said, "I'm not going to lose them."

"Oh. Erm, OK," I conceded, but Clackson was already streaking across the marble floor to the glass elevator.

One week passed. I heard nothing from Clackson. Two weeks. Still nothing. On the third week, I finally called the Standard.

"Newsdesk," a woman's voice said when I called.

"Oh, hello," I started nervously. "Is Stephen Clackson there please?"

"He's busy," said the woman, sounding impatient. "What's it about?"

"I came in to see Mr Clackson about a job, and I gave him my cuttings book and he said he would return it but I haven't heard anything yet," I said.

"Why didn't you give him a copy?" she asked.

"Well, he took the originals," I said, feeling stupid, "And the thing is, I don't care if you can't give me a job, I just need the cuttings back …"

"Hold on," the woman said.

The line went silent, clicked, rang again, and I heard Clackson's, cool, calm and collected voice say, "Mr Sykes. And how are you young man?"

"Er, not bad," I said, "The only thing is…"

"I know," he interrupted me. "Your cuttings. They seem to have got lost. Why don't you come in for a couple of weeks and see if you can find them?"

"Oh, OK, great, thanks," I said, totally flustered.

"I'll put you on to my secretary Karen Douglas."

The line went silent again, for longer this time, then clicked back to the woman I had been speaking to before.

"Hello, Tom," she said, sounding much friendlier. "9.30 on Monday OK?"

"Er, great," I said.

"See you then," she replied, and hung up.

And that's how I got my start in journalism. It turned out I could write, and my two weeks turned into a year.

I loved the *Standard*, not least because it was a drinkers' newspaper, and it was largely staffed by drunks. The first edition went out at 7.30am with a hangover and hair of the dog, and the last at about 4pm, with updates phoned in from the pub where we gathered every afternoon to gossip, bitch and drink away the day. One of the few exceptions was Clackson himself, who drank precisely one glass of wine a day at lunch and got to the office at 5.45 every morning.

Drinking was part of the job description and I embraced the booze culture of news wholeheartedly. The famous drinkers at the *Standard* were mainly men in their late forties or early fifties, hardened hacks like Colin Adamson or Richard Holliday, masters at turning around copy from a murder scene or abduction in a matter of minutes and filing on the spot – or, more frequently, from the nearest licensed purveyor of intoxicating liquor. Gervaise 'Barmy' Webb was another fixture at the local bar, Jimmy's, where he had an understanding with the bar staff that whenever he saw a cockroach he would dance a little jig to distract the customers in return for preferential, sometimes complimentary service. Barmy – as his name suggested – was such a strange guy that his suddenly breaking out into a two-step hardly seemed unusual.

Another pub we frequented, tucked away behind Kensington Church Road, was the Elephant. Every opportunity I got I would head to the Elephant, whose wood-panelled walls were adorned with famous front pages from the newspaper's history, for a session with Barmy, Colin or Richard, the *Standard*'s very own holy trinity of inebriation. I wanted what they had – a front page every week and a well-lubricated, first-name terms relationship with every bar girl for three square miles.

Colin – a tough, no-nonsense Scot, who suffered terribly from eczema – was a particularly prodigious drinker. He rolled into the office one day after lunch, saying, "God I'm plastered. I've had three pints."

I was confused. "Three pints Colin? That doesn't seem very much?"

"Aye – but they were pints o' wine," he replied, and sat down heavily in front of his screen to light one of the forty cigarettes he smoked daily and make his final adds to the front page of the last edition.

But the tides of change were running the other way. The Standard's drinking culture was dying out. The management were becoming less and less tolerant of the drunk gang, and increasing numbers of the new guard of reporters were earnest, swotty and square. They sat at their screens all day, typing furiously, and never had hangovers in the morning. I pitied them their serious, joyless existence, and determined never to be like them. Even when I crawled into the office at 5.30am, head pounding from another late night at the Elephant or Jimmy's, I held their sober lifestyles in contempt. After all, I could get through the day just fine, and I was getting more stories in the paper than them anyway.

I wasn't particularly popular at the *Standard*. The fact that I had simply waltzed into my job without paying my dues at the coalface of local journalism irritated a lot of the old school, working-class journalists who had done just that. I looked faintly like Clackson, too, so the other staff joked I was his secret love child, and that was why I had been given the job.

Email was still only a fledgling technology in our office in 1997, so we communicated using "on-screen inter-office memos". It was easy to find out what other people had messaged about you. I could never resist. One message that I remember said, "If that Tom pillock sits opposite me for much longer, he will find himself with considerably less space between his ears than he has at present."

But the pub had a magical bonding effect. The moment I sat down at a table in the Elephant with Colin, Richard or Barmy, I was part of the club; we all got along, united by beer, whisky and vodkas and tonic.

I loved hearing the drinking stories. Colin told me how he used to sleep all night on the bar-room floor at Harvey's on Fleet Street then go straight to work. Richard told me about drinking the East European liquor slivovitch in a bunker under Bosnian Serb mortar fire. "After a few hits of that you're like, 'Come on then, you bastards, give us your best shot'," explained Richard, standing in the middle of the pub and waggling his ass in the air.

My big break at the *Standard* came in a great disguise. A Swedish company had come out with tights for men. I posed in them, à la Christine Keeler, sitting backwards on a chair, and wrote 800 words to go with it.

The features head, Nicola Jeal, loved my piece, and she gave me more and more work. The piece on the tights was even used as part of the *Standard*'s ad campaign. Although I wasn't too happy about being plastered on bus stops and tube stations all over London in my tights, I was chuffed with the tagline, "The Best Writers are in the *Evening Standard*". So I couldn't take public transport for a few months. So what? I was getting somewhere.

The best thing about all this success was that I was earning a fortune. In a good week I could make over £1,000. I spent much of it in the pub, but I was spending more and more of my cash buying drugs – marijuana and, increasingly cocaine – from my dealer James.

I had first met James when I lived in Edinburgh, where he was also a student, and I used to buy weed off him. When we finished university and moved to London, James moved too. He lived in a musty, sparsely furnished house, and several nights a week I would drive over there in my beaten-up Fiat Panda, which Plum had given me, to score.

Over the years James had become much more than just a dealer – he had become one of my best friends. On the afternoons I didn't go to the pub I would race up to his house and sit in his garden smoking joints and waiting for the rest of our friends to finish work. We would spend hours smoking weed and throwing little twigs into the spiders' webs that covered his garden, watching with fascination as the spiders pounced on the twigs, cut them out of the webs so they fell to the ground and then swiftly patched up their insect traps and returned to the centre to wait for lunch.

The reason James became one of my best friends was, basically, because he was one of the few people who liked to smoke as much as me, and he always had some hash or skunk on him. Cocaine was great if I had the money because it meant I could drink all night without blacking out, and if I didn't have the cash, well, James usually had a package on him that he would let me dip into for free.

8

-2013 DAYS

SASHA WAS YOUNGER than me and she had another year at Edinburgh to go after I left. We split up, and hardly had any contact, but the following year she came to London from Dublin, where she was living, on her way to Greece where she was going for a month to visit a friend.

Sasha had chopped her long hair off and she was wearing a skirt over her jeans. She looked gorgeous and I fell back in love with her on the spot. Before the end of the night I had agreed to go and visit her for ten days in Greece to coincide with my twenty-fifth birthday. I had several weeks of holiday time from the *Standard* that I wanted to use up, so the trip made perfect sense.

And so it was that I woke up the day after my birthday in a cheap but clean hotel on the Greek island of Paxos, with last night's ouzo banging noxiously around my head and a faint smell of charred bacon in the air.

My eyes hardly open, I reached out my hand to grab the bottle of water by our bed and took a gulp. Something solid hit my tongue and I sprayed water all over the room in disgust. I knew instantly what it was. The soaked, decomposing cigarette butt lay on the floor and I groaned in disgust.

Sasha opened her eyes.

"What is it?" she asked.

"There was a fag butt in the water and I just took a gulp," I said.

"Eughh. You poor thing," said Sasha.

We lay there a few minutes. "We've got to get up," I said. "We've got to check out of here by 12."

"What time is it now?"

I checked my watch. "11. How you feeling?"

"Uggh," said Sasha in reply. "What did we do last night?"

"I don't know. I remember being in that bar drinking ouzo, then I think I had an argument with the barman about the bill. I can't really remember after that."

We lay back in silence for a few moments more. A bell clanged arhythmically near our room as a goat outside munched grass. Fucking goats.

"Come on then," I said, hauling myself into a sitting position on the edge of the bed. "Let's do it."

We must have been halfway through packing our stuff when Sasha started pulling the twisted sheet straight on the bed.

"You don't have to make the bed," I said, irritated at the delay. "We're leaving, aren't we … *shit*."

We were both staring at the bedsheet, which had two big, black-edged holes burnt through it.

"Shit," I said again. The blood was pumping to my head. So that's what the burning smell was. I must have fallen asleep with a lit cigarette. We were lucky to be alive.

"Oh my god, Tommy, this really is not funny," said Sasha sitting down heavily on the bed again. She rifled through the rumpled sheets and plucked out a half-burned cigarette. Thank god it had gone out.

"You really can't smoke in bed when you are so pissed," Sasha said. She reached out for her socks and was just about to put them on, when she stopped and said, "What's that?"

I sat down next to her on the bed. Sasha had a huge angry blister on her shin. It looked like a burn.

"It looks like a burn," she said.

"Oh my god I am so sorry," I said.

"I can't believe you got so pissed you burnt a hole in my leg as well as nearly burning up the bed," said Sasha, her eyes bright with tears.

"It was an accident!" I said.

I got up and stalked off angrily to the bathroom. I looked at myself in the mirror. You idiot, I thought. I shouted through to the other room, "Anyway, you're no better. I can't believe you were so pissed you didn't wake up although your leg was on fire."

I showered in pained silence. I dried off and went back to the bedroom. Sasha was sitting on the bed looking dumbly at the blister.

"I'm sorry," I whispered as I kissed her gently. "Really, I am so sorry."

"That's okay," sighed Sasha. "I guess you're right. It's my fault as well."

"I've branded you," I tried. "You're mine forever now."

9

-1631 DAYS

IN 1998 I JOINED the *Daily Telegraph* as a trainee, but by the end of 1999 it was clear they weren't going to give me a full-time job. I had argued with the news desk too often, and then there was the time there was a flu bug going round and I called in sick for a week, used the time to get stoned and paint my room above the kebab shop yellow, and then actually did get sick the following week. Also, I was annoyed, after the success I had had at the *Standard*, that I wasn't being given more feature-writing opportunities. I went back to the *Standard* in 2000, aged twenty-six, as a fully paid-up member of staff.

But what was I going to write about? The news desk handed out general assignments, but to really shine reporters had to develop a specialty topic.

I sounded out Colin and Richard over a few beers at the Elephant one afternoon.

"Write what you know," they both said. What did I like doing?

What did I know? I knew drugs and alcohol. What did I like doing? I liked partying and going out.

"So there's your answer," said Colin. I was going to write about youth culture in London in all its varied forms. I was going to stay out late and cover the party beat.

My first big assignment was to cover the Glastonbury festival in Somerset for the paper – the scene of my acid-fuelled, out-of-body teenage experience.

I picked up my pass from Karen on the news desk, and when I opened the official-looking envelope I realised with delight that I had been given an extra guest pass for a friend. It was a no-brainer who I would take. It had to be James, who, in return for a free ticket would sort me out with all the E, coke and weed I required.

I rang him and proposed the deal.

"Yeah, sure," said James. "What time do we leave?" Another great thing about James was that because he never had to go to work he was always available for impetuous, last-minute road trips.

Driving up to Glastonbury, James stashed his drugs all around the car that the *Standard* had rented for me. We had seven grams of coke, fifteen pills and an ounce of hash, which James hid down various seat-backs and ventilation slots. He needn't have bothered. We showed our media passes, and they let us drive in without a search.

The festival began on a Friday. There was no newspaper

at the weekends, as the *Standard* was strictly a commuter title. That meant all I would have to do was file a round-up story on Sunday night for Monday morning. I swore to myself I wouldn't get too wasted before then.

I popped a pill or two on the Friday and Saturday nights, nothing too excessive, and on Sunday, I stayed sober while David Bowie played the main stage. I wrote up my report of the weekend and called the news desk to phone it in.

"Good job, thanks Tom," the night editor said when I had finished. I felt a surge of relief that I had done my job. Now I could get down to the serious business of getting bombed.

I found James dancing to a sound system playing trance outside a blanket stall called Joe Bananas.

"I'm done," I shouted in his ear. "Give us a pill."

James bounced up and down on the spot, wrapped in a blanket. "I can't mate. I've got rid of them all," he said.

I looked at him in shocked amazement, then exploded.

"You what?" I screamed at him. "You fucking cunt. I can't believe I brought you here, got you in and everything, and you didn't even save one fucking pill for me."

"Sorry mate," he said. "I sold the last one for five quid to get some cash to buy a hot dog."

"To buy a fucking hot dog?" I shouted, panicking badly. "There's free fucking hot dogs in the press tent you wanker. Stop fucking dancing."

James was reaching down into his shoe. He pulled out a little plastic bag with three pills in it. He was grinning at me.

"Tommy, Tommy," he laughed, waving the bag in front of my face. "I'm only joking mate. Course I saved some for tonight. I'm only winding you up. Ha ha ha!"

I felt the relief surge over me. I hugged James and he hugged me back. "You bastard," I said. He took one of the pills out and handed it to me, mimicking me, saying, "A fucking hot dog!"

I smiled at him and then looked at the pill in my hand. It looked like one of those tiny mints they give you tins of free in the smarter hotels, but thicker, with rough, crumbly edges. I tapped a guy dancing next to me with a bottle of water on the shoulder.

"Can I borrow your water, mate," I asked, making the drinking sign. He nodded and passed me the bottle. I washed the pill down with a glug of liquid.

Just before I came up, I thought fleetingly about how pathetically grateful I was that James had actually saved a few pills for me. If he hadn't had them, my whole weekend would have been ruined. And he knew it. I hated it when James played these power games with drugs. He did it with a smile on his face, and it was all a big joke, but it was totally fucked up. He wanted me to be grateful. He wanted to see me lose it, or beg, *beg* for the drugs. He was a…

The soundtrack of complaints in my head stopped as the pill kicked in. I shut my eyes and rolled my eyes back in my head. I ran my hand through my hair and it felt like straw. That was a sure sign I was coming up.

The DJ was playing a classic tune. The keyboards sounded like searchlights in my ears. The crowd threw its hands in the air and everyone was dancing with me. I started feeling sick but I knew to ignore it. I threw up but my puke looked and tasted like gold. Then I was dancing. "Put your hands in the air," yelled the DJ. I hugged James. "I love you man. These pills are wicked. I love you man."

At four in the morning James and I were finally coming down. We were sitting on the grass around a fire somewhere at the top of the Glastonbury site, smoking joints and drinking beers. I had just spent half an hour chatting to a man whose face was covered in thick, werewolf-like hair. I was so wasted I had asked him about it without any reservations, and he had told me he was from a family of gypsies. In Eastern Europe, where they'd originally come from, the family were feared and revered as supernatural beings.

James and I kept wandering from one fire to the next, sitting down for a bit, skinning up and smoking joints. The smoke felt amazing in my lungs, clear, purifying.

"Amazing pills man," I said, for maybe the thirty-fourth time.

"Tommy, would I ever let you down," grinned James. Then he did his impression of me again that he'd been doing all night, "A fucking hot dog".

"Shut up you wanker," I said.

We started talking to some hippies who had been attracted by the smell of grass and were desperate for a hit on our joint. James and I teased them, skinning up and passing the joint back and forth between us while the hippies kept trying to be smart and funny and ingratiating in the hope we would give them a hit. We didn't. The power games were fun when you were the one who was holding.

At 5am, as we sat there wild-eyed, smoking pot, still buzzing from the E, James got out his coke. I was in the middle of taking a sniff when my phone rang. I pulled it out in horror and stared at it.

"Who is that?" James asked.

I knew who it was. I flipped open the phone. Before I could speak Karen was barking down my ear, "Hello, Tom, could you hold while I put you over to Clackson? Thanks."

Shit shit shit.

Clackson came on the line. "Hello, Mr Sykes. Sorry to wake you so early, young man, but I need you to re-nose your Glasto copy," he was talking very fast and sounded very, very sober. His voice sounded like it was coming from a million miles away.

"Sure," I said, gesturing madly at James and the hippies to shut up. "What do you need?"

Stephen sounded annoyed that I had to ask. "You know, Tom. The usual. What's going on now. What can you actually *see* right now?"

What I could see was James waving a massive spliff under my nose and shrugging at me as a crowd of hippies berated him for a hit on it like a scene out of *Dawn of the Dead*.

"Erm, well," I said. "I don't know, erm, just lots of people packing up to leave and..."

Stephen cut me off. "Just file, OK?"

The line went dead. I sat in the grass scribbling on a bit of old napkin with a pencil I found in my pocket. All the hippies kept coming up and asking, "What are you writing, man? What's going on?"

I shouted over to James that we had to find somewhere quieter, that I had to re-write the first few paragraphs. We got up and ran across the field trying to find a quiet spot. It was like being stuck in a computer game designed by MC Escher. Everywhere we went was the same, just people trekking through the mud. Eventually I sat down on the grass and tried not to cry.

"James, just try and keep these people away from me for ten minutes OK? Please?"

I sat down and started to write. As I cobbled together a few lines, James stood over me in the breaking dawn, fending off inquiries from curious, stoned passers-by who were all wanting to know what I was doing. After fifteen minutes he just pretended to be crazy and violent and shouted at anyone who came near, "Just fuck off, OK?" like some obscene – but highly efficient – talking guard dog. It's only a matter of time before he starts barking, I thought.

Just as I got the sentences together the desk rang again.

"Hold for Stephen please," said Karen.

She put me through. "OK, ready to go?" asked Stephen.

"Sure," I said as confidently as I could. "Do you want to patch me through to copy?"

"No, we're out of time. I'll take it."

Oh shit. This was bad. My throat was dry and my voice cracking as I read my pitiful sentences out to Stephen. I heard his keyboard clacking down the line and then halfway through the keyboard sound just stopped. When I finished, Stephen waited. And waited. And waited.

"Is that it?" he asked finally.

"Erm, yeah…" I said.

"What's going on Tom?" he asked. "This isn't difficult."

"Sorry, I think I must be sleepy. Just got up."

"You just got up?" Stephen said. "Really?"

"Erm, well, yeah, I haven't actually been to bed yet."

Oh Christ. Why did I say that? Another long pause.

"Tom," said Stephen. "I'll do this for you. Get some sleep and call when you wake up." The phone went dead. My face was white.

James was in hysterics. "I can't believe you just had to file. Look at the fucking state of you."

I couldn't say anything. I wanted to cry. Was I going to be fired? I looked at James and I hated him. Hated his drugs. Hated the way he had tricked me into taking them. Fucking dealer cunt.

"Skin up," I said.

And so James and I sat there in the dawn's early light surveying the wreckage of the festival, smoking joint after joint after joint.

The thing I liked about smoking dope was that it just made everything bad go away. So Clackson was a little pissed off with me. So what? What did they expect? It was Glastonbury. I was twenty-six. This is what journalists were *supposed* to do, wasn't it? This was the whole point.

Later that day James and I packed up our tent and drove back to London. At the Chiswick roundabout on the approach into London an orange-vested peddler was selling copies of the *Standard*. Even from a distance I could make out the picture of Bowie on the main stage and in big capital letters on the front page three words that made everything all right: "BY TOM SYKES".

Everything had turned out nice again.

10

-1208 DAYS

i GOT AWAY with the Glastonbury debacle because Stephen basically wrote the story for me. I was Stephen's protégé, after all, so he took care of me. But the following year, he retired, and the new guy who took over his desk had none of Stephen's indulgence.

On the very last day of August 2001, I was fired from the *Standard*. The official reason was cutbacks, but coincidentally the axe fell just after I got the name of a friend of the editor wrong in a piece I wrote for the paper. It wasn't just any old friend – it was the actor Richard Harris. I wrote Robert Harris for some reason, and the mistake wasn't noticed until the paper was out on the stands, with a huge story accompanied by full colour pictures on the prized page three spot about how "Robert Harris" was going to be the star of the *Harry Potter* films. It still makes me cringe.

When I was called into the editor's office, I knew I was

about to get whacked. It was like that horrible last day at Eton all over again. It was inevitable that I was going to mess up a crucial detail like this eventually. I was smoking a lot of skunk – super-strong grass grown under artificial lights – with James most nights and my brain rarely de-fogged during the day.

Sure enough, I was told to go. But because of my staff contract, I was offered a handsome pay-off. I could hardly believe it. Where did I sign?

I couldn't have been happier as I strolled out of the offices of the *Evening Standard* for the last time, declining even to pack up my desk. Drunk on bravado, I wasn't worried in the least about my long-term situation. I would go freelance. I was twenty-seven, and I knew I was a good writer when I focused. I'd just have to stop smoking so much damn pot. I raced up to see James and tell him the news over a few joints.

I didn't actually need much money, I told James, as he congratulated me on my pay-off and tossed me a big bag of sweet-smelling buds. I had just bought a little house in Golborne Road, just up the street from Notting Hill Gate, with my three sisters, Alice, Lucy and Plum. We had bought it with money that my granny had given to us in trust when we were children, and the payments on the mortgage we had needed on top of the lump sum were just a couple of hundred pounds a month. I could easily cover that with my pay-off. For my sisters, who had all moved to New York, it was an investment. For Sasha and I, who got to live there for next to nothing, it was a dream come true.

Sasha and I had been living together for over a year now. We both had the same idea of a good time – going out to the pub and meeting up with mates for a slew of pints. Once I got fired, though, Sasha did start to get a bit annoyed that she had to get up at seven every morning to get to work – Sasha had a job designing the interiors of shops – while I lay in bed sleeping off my hangover.

I was the world's worst freelance journalist. In the first week after I got fired I wrote a witty piece about the upside of being fired (*"The Joy of Sack"*). It was the only piece I wrote in three months. I never sold it.

I was sitting at the kitchen table going through the piece yet again on the afternoon of September 11, when the Twin Towers fell in New York. Once I got through to my sisters in New York, I went up to James's, and spent every day of the next fortnight there watching the World Trade Centre crumble over and over again on TV, smoking grass and drinking tea before meeting up with Sasha for beers in the evening.

After two weeks I set about trying to sell my piece, figuring that the papers might be in need of something other than gloom and doom. I couldn't have been more wrong.

"Give it a couple of months, Tom," one short-tempered editor told me. "Nobody really gives a shit about you getting fired right now."

September dragged into October. There was still no

work for my stock in trade – light, fluffy articles about nothing – so I didn't bother looking. I spent a lot of time at James's, and he spent a lot of time at mine.

One night Sasha got home from work to find me, stoned again, lying on the sofa listening to Pink Floyd, munching chocolate and drinking diet Coke.

She turned off the stereo and sat down next to me.

"Monkey, I'm really getting scared," she started.

I sat up and tried to concentrate, but my head was swimming.

"Why?" I asked.

"Because you haven't had any work since you got fired," she said. "What are we going to do?"

"It's not like I haven't been trying, Sasha," I snapped defensively. "There isn't any work. No one's commissioning anything."

"Well maybe if you didn't go and hang out with your other *girlfriend* James and get stoned in his garden all day, you'd be able to find some."

"Look, babe, it's fine, don't worry about it. I've still got all that money from the *Standard*. Don't stress. Things just aren't good at the moment."

"Well, if you are just going to sit around all day maybe you could at least try and tidy up after yourself then," she said, standing up, picking up the empty sweet wrappers and drink cans around me. She didn't touch the newspaper with rolling papers and clumps of grass and torn-up bits of cardboard scattered over it.

The next day, a little shocked by Sasha's outburst,

because Sasha and I never argued, I rang Toby Young, a friend and journalist who had been fired from almost every newspaper in the UK. He had a look at the "*Joy of Sack*" piece for me, and suggested I send it to a contact of his at *GQ* magazine.

I duly emailed the article off and fifteen minutes later got a reply from the Features Editor, Alex Bilmes. The piece was great, very smart and funny, he said. He didn't want it, he said. But there was a job open at *GQ* for an Assistant Features Editor. Was I interested?

Two weeks later, scrubbed, shaved and with a full forty-eight hours between me and my last joint I was sitting at a table in the subdued light of the bar in Claridge's hotel in Mayfair with Alex while the deputy editor, Bill Prince, went to get a round of Bloody Marys. It was five in the afternoon.

Bill was wearing an immaculate two-piece Savile Row suit from the same tailor as me, Kilgour, which I felt could only be a good omen. The three of us exchanged pleasantries for a few minutes, and then I asked what they were looking for. "Well," said Bill, "We want someone who can manage the front section of the magazine and go out every night as well. We need someone to be our eyes and ears on the ground. If tricorn hats are suddenly hot, we want you to know about it and get it in the magazine first."

Go out every night and look for hats? I could do that, I assured them. I got the job.

Once again, I reflected with some satisfaction, I had

turned it around. Sasha was delighted, and I was getting away with it.

11

-1124 DAYS

I STARTED AT *GQ* in the middle of November. My first outburst of public drunkenness came in December, when we had the annual Christmas lunch. I strode into the boardroom at about 12.30 for my first glass of champagne, and ran straight into the guest of honour, disgraced politician Neil Hamilton and his self-described battleaxe of a wife, Christine. Their luck had run low after Neil had been thrown out of the government, and he and his wife had been reduced to the role of the nation's court jesters, humiliating themselves for money. Their latest stunt had been to pose naked in *GQ* – a revoltingly distasteful sight as they were both in their fifties, flabby from too many years spent with their snouts in the trough, but the stunt had garnered mountains of attention for the magazine in the papers. And if there was one thing our editor, Dylan Jones, cared about, it was getting attention from the papers.

I was chatting to Neil about his disastrous career when I began to notice that he was literally tipping glass after glass of champagne down his neck. The man was going to be slaughtered. I paced myself by him. For every two glasses he had, I drank just one.

Four glasses for me and eight for him later, we sat down to eat. The lights were dimmed and we were served smoked salmon, turkey and Christmas pudding. There was also a lot of wine. Somewhere round about the middle of the lunch I began to notice that I was feeling very, very drunk. Luckily I had taken out some insurance against this and scored a wrap of coke off James the night before. I went to the bathroom and did a line, and returned to the table reassuringly clear-headed. Another glass of wine? Why not?

At the end of lunch our managing editor, Claire, started handing out presents. I can't remember what I got. Miles, the art editor, was given a pair of hair clippers.

"Anyone want their hair cut?" he shouted, more in hope than expectation.

Why do I do these things? Why do I do them? I felt my hand going up. And I was shouting, "Yeah me! Me! Me!"

"Really?' asked Miles.

"Sure," I shouted. "I need a hair cut."

-1097 DAYS

I WOKE UP the next morning and groaned deeply. Sasha had already gone to work. The alarm clock showed 9am. I had to get a move on. What the hell had I done last night? I couldn't remember a thing.

I staggered through to the bathroom to brush my teeth and looked in the mirror.

So *that* was what had happened. My head was shaved. Not totally bald, but there couldn't have been more than one-tenth of an inch of hair left.

I ran a bath. A hot bath. The sweating would help me to detox. So I was going to be late today. So what.

I lay in the bath with my eyes closed and the day before started to come back to me. Miles with his hair clippers. Me sitting on the chair. Everyone standing around, watching, cheering me on.

At least someone had been more embarrassing than me. I had a vague memory of Neil Hamilton ripping open his shirt and demanding one of the girls at the office shave his chest hair. But then again, Neil Hamilton didn't work at *GQ*. He didn't have to go into the office this morning. He wasn't the new boy, who had only been working there a month and should have been trying to make a good impression. Shit shit shit.

I was an idiot, and a piss head, and now everybody knew it. My haircut would make sure they didn't forget.

Although my hair grew back a little over Christmas, my reputation never really recovered. I tried not to mind. So people thought I was a crazy drunk guy. Well, I was. That was the whole point of being me, right? That was my brand. Although, I reflected, it would have been nice if my editors at my new job had thought that I was smart, intelligent, funny and witty instead of just plain deranged.

I was on a three-month probation period at *GQ*, so when I got back to work in the New Year I did get serious for a little while. I cut right back on the drinking and smoked almost no dope in the week, and when the three months were up Dylan called me into his office and told me I was doing well, and to keep it up. "You've got opportunities to move up the masthead here," he told me. This was not strictly true as neither the features editor, Alex, and especially not Dylan or Bill were about to leave, so actually there wasn't really anywhere to go, but I thanked him anyway.

My main job at *GQ* was to edit the front section of the magazine, *Details*, which covered all the things I liked, such as music, clubs, fashion, nightlife, food, parties and alcohol. Most nights there were events or parties to go to, and as the year wore on I was out later and later every night. I would go to the event, then, once it had finished head off to a pub to meet my friends, Olly, Frank, another university buddy who lived in the same part of west London, and usually James.

Often when I got home late at night, Sasha would be asleep, and when she left for work I would be crashed out. We could go for days at a time just communicating by phone.

I had bought a small Vespa motorbike to replace Plum's Fiat Panda – I had sold the car to James for two ounces of skunk and a gram of coke – and I could get from Golborne Road to the Condé Nast offices near Oxford Circus in twelve minutes flat. I had to be there by 9.30 in the morning, and I usually made it by 9.45. Alex didn't mind me being late but Bill had a thing about lateness.

One morning after a particularly heavy night I didn't get in until 11am. I sat down at my desk and sent Bill an email.

"Sorry I am so late," I wrote, "My bike wouldn't start and I had to get a bus. Then the bus broke down in Notting Hill and I had to get a cab."

One second. Two seconds. Three seconds. Bing! "Did the cab break down as well?"

I stared intently at my screen for a few minutes until I couldn't take it anymore. I went outside for a smoke and Alex followed me. We stood outside the building smoking in silence in the pale English sun. The cigarette tasted stale in my hungover mouth. I felt like shit.

Eventually I spoke. "So I guess Bill copied you in on that little exchange," I said.

"Yup," said Alex.

"Am I going to get fired?" I asked.

"No don't be stupid of course you're not going to get fired, Tom," said Alex. Then he gave me the talk. "Bill and Dylan trust me to run the features desk, and I understand that you have to go out every night. But you will get fired if it carries on and you don't pull your weight. I like you

Tom, and you're a great guy, but I can only plead your case so far. Everyone likes you, but you are losing their respect as a journalist. Just sort out the section."

I went back in and sat at my desk, avoiding eye contact with Bill all day. The section was a mess. None of the copy was in. When work ended I went to the pub. Then I got on the bike, and sped up to James's for a joint.

James's house was like a social club for me and my friends. Most of us would pass through at some stage of the evening to pick up a packet of powder or herbs, and stay around for a joint and a cup of tea.

-835 DAYS

THE MOST EAGERLY anticipated event of the year at *GQ* was the conference. In 2002 we were given the run of a country-house hotel in Wiltshire for the annual piss-up. It was a two-day event, but I missed the first night because I was in New York visiting my sisters.

We spent the day doing corporate bonding type events like clay pigeon shooting and riding three wheelers through the mud-sodden countryside. But the party in the evening was what it was really all about.

One moment I was having a glass of wine with Peter Stewart, the publisher, the next I was tired and hungry and curling up in bed. I woke up in the morning with a stinking headache an apple core in my bed and an uncomfortable feeling that my behaviour hadn't been all it might have the night before.

I got out of bed and looked around for my suitcase. That was when I realised I wasn't in my own room. I was in a girl's room. All my clothes were scattered on the floor. I was naked. Oh shit.

I was quite alone in the room, so I took a shower and tried to remember what I had done the night before. Despite being a drunken fool, I was proud of the fact I had never cheated on Sasha, and I just had a gut feeling I hadn't done anything really bad.

Oddly, the fact that I was naked in a bed not my own didn't concern me too much as I washed and conditioned my hair in the shower to help get rid of the booze smell. It was part of a pattern. Lately, when I had been really drunk, I had developed a thing about climbing naked into other people's beds. It always amazed me that I did this, as, sober, I am a prude. I hate other people seeing me naked. It was one of the main reasons I never went to the gym. All that locker-room stuff gave me the creeps.

But over the past few months I had climbed into bed first with my friends Hugh and Sarah, and then with another couple Tom and Minnie. Apparently when they asked what I was doing, I would say things like, "But you look so comfy! I just want to cuddle up," and then pass out. Between them.

Still, I figured as I used the complimentary-sized bottle of mouthwash by the sink to help freshen up my breath in lieu

of a toothbrush, it was a shame it had happened at the conference. With work people. I had no idea where my room was
so I dressed in last night's shirt, and went down to breakfast.

When I walked into the dining room thirty faces from
the office turned towards me and simultaneously laughed at
me with friendly contempt. This had been bad, then. I put
my arms by my side to shrug as if to say, "*What me?*" and
smiled knowingly, as if I knew exactly what I had done. No
one seemed angry, at least, just highly amused by my antics.
I got my coffee and walked over to sit with Alex and Helen,
a tall, funny, blonde girl who worked in the art department.

"Alright Sykesy," said Alex as I sat down. "Sleep well?"

"Yeah," I said as I took a sip of coffee. "Why?"

"Do you remember what you did last night Tom?"
Helen asked me, grinning from ear to ear.

"No, but I suspect I am about to find out," I smiled,
trying to be fearless and smooth.

"Well, you were really drunk, and you came into my
room," Helen said, in her matter-of-fact way. I noticed that
all the other staff were now craning around our table to
listen. Clearly this wasn't the first time this story had been
told this morning. "Then you took all your clothes off and
climbed into my bed," Helen continued. "So I got out of
the bed and tried to get rid of you, but you wouldn't leave.
You just kept saying, 'Let me sleep, let me sleep.' Then you
picked up one of my tampons and started taking it apart.
And I was like, 'Tom, leave now!' but you wouldn't and you
reached out to the fruit bowl and grabbed an apple and

started eating it. You were just like, 'I'm hungry!' and that was when I left to go and sleep in Millie's room."

Helen was grinning at me uncontrollably. Everyone listening was laughing at me. I was drenched in shame and embarrassment. I fought to find the magic phrase. But, this time, it didn't come. The best I could do was, "And you say I was eating an *apple*?"

-675 DAYS

t HE BED-CRASHING incident at the conference became a mini *GQ* legend. For weeks afterwards, people would come up to me apropos of nothing and say in the most shocked and outraged tone they could muster, "An *apple* you say? Are you *quite sure*?"

The bottom line was that *GQ* stood as much for drunken debauchery as it did for £2,000 suits and cashmere socks. I heard countless times what a great and friendly guy one former editor called Michael VerMeulen was, before I learned that he died of a cocaine overdose at the ripe old age of thirty-eight. In a documentary about Britpop, James Brown, who had been the *GQ* editor before Dylan, declared that the bathroom was his boardroom, and the most important deals when he was editor of *GQ* were struck over lines of weasel dust. Brown was fired after he oversaw an issue that declared Rommel to be the century's 41st most stylish

man, much to the disgust of Condé Nast's Jewish propri-
etors, the Newhouse family. He had never checked the issue
and had no idea about the inclusion of the Nazi. After he
was fired, he came back to the office saying, "Who put
Rommel in?" (It was one of the art editors.)

But the drinking and partying began to impinge more
seriously on my capacity to do the job. The front section was
a mess. The copy was always late for two reasons. Firstly, the
writers who were supposed to be working for me didn't
respect me – they were all friends of friends appointed by Bill
and Dylan and only answered to them. Secondly, when the
copy came in, I would sigh deeply and bang my already-sore
head on the desk and then go outside for a cigarette and a
coffee rather than start processing it through the system.

As the situation got worse I became more and more
desperate to get to the pub after work (although, unlike one
of my predecessors in the same job, at least I wasn't actually
going to the pub in the daytime). Alex and Bill would hardly
come to the pub with me anymore, and when they did, they
didn't get drunk, so I started hanging out with the art
department who loved to drink, and drank properly.

My excuses were getting worse. One night I went for
dinner at Nobu with Toby Young who was writing a piece
about London Fashion Week for British *Vogue*. After dinner,
we went to a nightclub event that was being held for a music
business awards show. At the door they asked who I was,
and I declared I was Alex James, the bassist in the band Blur.
"This is my … entourage," I winked cheekily at the clip-

board-wielding hot blonde on the door, putting on a David Bowie voice and pointing to my seven pals.

"Oh, please, come in," she flirted back cheekily to me.

We made it to the bar and ordered vodka and tonics, and I reflected on just how calmly I had pretended to be someone else to get us all in. I had done it without really thinking. It just showed how far a little confidence could go. I was, actually, pretty cool.

-674 DAYS

NORMAL DRINKERS don't really understand how blackouts work. Sure, the first bit is easy to understand – one moment you're questioning whether impersonating trendy bassists is a valid way to get into a party, the next you are waking up in a sweaty bed. You have no memory of what has happened in between. The memory chip has been wiped.

But you rack your brains. You were with Toby at Nobu, right, drinking sake. Then the party, where you pretended to be Alex James (very funny). Then I remember the bar ... nope, nothing. Sasha had already gone to work so I couldn't ask her. Actually, it seemed kind of late. Where the hell was the clock? Shit shit shit. Down to the kitchen. And there's the clock on the cooker. 11.45AM. SHIT! You were supposed to be at work two hours ago! Shitting hell!

Okay, the only thing to do was to pretend I was sick. I rang Alex on his mobile. He answered on the first half ring. "Tom? Where are you?"

"Hey man, I'm sorry I haven't called. I'm sick. I went for dinner at Nobu last night and I think I must have eaten a bad bit of sushi."

Silence.

"Alex?"

"Don't move."

Then I heard Alex get up from his desk, clomp his way down the corridor, down the stairs, into the street. The spark of a lighter. The crackle of burning tobacco. Then Alex saying to me, "Tom, is this some kind of fucking joke?"

"What? No man. I just feel really shit. I'm not hungover, I promise," I said, pacing the kitchen.

"You're not hungover?"

"No, man. Bad sushi."

"Okay, firstly Tom, they don't fucking *do* bad sushi at Nobu, and secondly, you were on the phone to me, ooh, let's see, five hours and fifteen minutes ago!"

Oh shit. Hot and cold. The clock said 11.47. "What?" I said. I still had no memory.

"For Christ's sake Tom you were on the phone to me. I had to leave my phone on all night because I was expecting a call from LA. And at four am, you ring. And you're yelling at me, *yelling* Tom, 'Bilmes, you fucker, get your ass down here now you wanker.' So I tell you to get lost," – on the other end of the phone I collapse onto the sofa and – too late – it all starts coming back. I was at that record party doing coke! Shit! Alex is not screaming in my ear, like I would be (and apparently was just a few hours before), he sounds bemused and upset more than angry – "And then you call again at five and again at fucking *six-thirty* to *apologise* for calling before." OK, now he's screaming, "I'm your boss Tom! I'm your boss. *And you're calling me to tell me how many Es you've done!*"

There's a long silence while all the memories flood back to me. "Alex, I can't work today. I'm sorry. I really am sorry."

"Sorry doesn't mean anything, Tom, if you just go out and do the same thing over and over and over again." And the line went dead.

-645 DAYS

IT DIDN'T TAKE a psychic to see that sooner or later I was going to get fired from *GQ*. The magazine and I were suffering from mutual contempt. They thought I was useless, and were probably right. I was angry with them because they hadn't run a column I had written about getting engaged to Sasha, which had happened at the end of the year. And boy, was I drinking and smoking a lot of weed.

I was sitting at my desk one day when the phone rang. It was Bridget, my sister's room-mate in New York.

"Hi Tommy," she said. "Are you still interested in working out here?"

I had had a twenty-second conversation with her the last time I was in New York about maybe working at the *New York Post,* where she worked. I looked around the *GQ* offices where everyone hated me and wouldn't even run my engagement column. "Sure," I said.

"Well, the features editor at the *Post*, Faye Penn, is looking for someone like you," Bridget said. What do you mean someone like me, I thought, but didn't say. I knew what she meant anyway. Someone young, sharp and bright. Basically the non-drunk, non-high version of me that I was so good at pretending to be when I needed to. "Are you interested?"

Three weeks later I walked into Dylan's office and announced my resignation. I was going to New York. I've never seen a man look so relieved. The next week I gave a leaving speech in which I jestingly apologised to Dylan for having conned him into hiring me, and Dylan jestingly gave a speech saying that if it didn't work out in New York, I could always come back to London and "work at *Esquire*". What a joker!

It was actually a good night. By quitting, I had solved the biggest problem the magazine had faced in the past year and everyone was relieved that I had jumped before I was pushed.

As for New York, I thought to myself, as I danced the night away with Sasha, at a nearby bar I had hired for my leaving party, I only knew one thing. I had to cut back on the drink and the drugs or I wasn't going to last five minutes.

12

-605 DAYS

EFORE I LEFT for America, I wanted to take Sasha to see my dad. She had never met him before.

I called Dad up and arranged a meeting at a Mayfair wine bar. It was a warm early-summer evening, and Sasha and I were crazed trying to finish packing up the house, which I had sold, making a good profit for me and my sisters. We had ended up with about £40,000 each.

I rode into town on the Vespa with Sasha on the back. Even though this was supposed to be "a quick drink", I had a hunch I was almost certain to drink too much to ride the bike home and would have to leave it locked to a lamp post overnight. It was just impossible not to drink when you were with my dad.

Sasha and I walked into the bar and there he was, sitting round a wooden table with three of his cronies.

"Aha," my dad said as we walked in, leaping to his feet. "Welcome, welcome."

"Hi Dad," I said, and gave him a hug, which was what I usually did because it just felt easier to pretend that a hug was normal rather than do what I really felt like, which was shake hands. "How's it going?"

"Not bad, not bad," he said. "Drink?" Then he looked at Sasha, "Drink?"

Sasha was looking confused and tried to smile. Everything always seemed to happen quite fast when my dad was involved. "Erm, sure ..." she was saying.

I stepped in, "Sasha, this is my dad, Dad, this is Sasha, my fiancée."

"What do you want?" Dad was asking her.

"We'll both have a pint of lager, please Dad," I cut in, trying to take some of the pressure off Sasha.

"Filthy fucking lager!" he exclaimed in disgust. "Well, sit down and I'll go and get them for you. Are you sure you wouldn't prefer a nice glass of champagne?"

"No, thanks Dad, a beer will be fine."

He shrugged, made a face of hopelessness, and indicated the three cronies sitting there with him.

"This is Thomas," he said, pointing toward a very red, portly old gentleman sitting to his right, and then, turning to a skinny, weasel-faced man on his left, "And this is Patrick. Patrick used to be an IRA hitman so watch what you say or he'll kill you."

"OK, will do," I said as brightly as possible and sat down next to him and smiled.

The third guy – a middle-aged, well-fed man in a suit – then said, "Hey? Aren't you going to introduce me?"

"Of course I am," said Dad. "This is Alexander Nikrassov. He's a very prominent Russian so you have to be reasonably guarded what you say around him as well."

Sasha and I sat down to talk to this unlikely trio while Dad went and got us drinks at the bar. I was a little thrown as I had been expecting that Sasha and I would meet him on his own. I guess I'd been making the mistake – again – of hoping we could have some kind of sensible conversation. These people, I reflected, were insurance against that.

"So, er, how long ago did you get out of the IRA?" I asked the hitman. He gave a mean smile and promptly changed the subject.

Conversation got easier after several pints. Thomas was ranting on about how the European Union was a giant conspiracy and the Euro was an evil plot to ruin us all and steal all our money, masterminded by Tony Blair. Nikrassov talked enthusiastically about the financial opportunities afforded by the break-up of the Soviet Union. Dad was doing his usual conversational patter, quoting Shakespeare and Ovid while running through a quick history of modern civilisation.

The weird thing about seeing my dad was that although he was undoubtedly there, being charming and funny in his own way, I could never seem to get him to actually engage in the present situation. This time, for example, he didn't ask me anything about the wedding, or why we were moving to New York, which, after all, was the reason we had come to see him.

Eventually I tried to prompt him, "So, erm, Dad, you know we are moving to New York and getting married, don't you?"

"Yes, yes," he said enthusiastically. "God, I loved New York when I was younger."

Thomas bellowed across the table, "I have never seen such horrendous poverty as I have seen in America, anywhere. Not in the Third World, India, Africa, never have I seen deprivation like America."

Everybody looked at him for a few seconds and then tried to return to their own conversations.

I remembered my dad going to New York a lot when I was aged seven or so. His circle of friends ranged from Claus von Bulow to Charlie Schultz. I remembered a story about the time he arrived in New York right after Black Wednesday, the 1987 stockmarket crash, and was hanging out with a Texan billionaire who had been identified that morning as one of the six individuals who had lost over $1bn in the crash.

"He was holed up in the top floor of the Carlyle with Bobby Short playing the piano downstairs," my dad said. "When I asked him what it was like to lose a billion dollars, his only comment was that it might be a good time to try and buy *Time-Life*. He said the neon clock on their building was a bit bright, and if he bought it he would be able to turn the clock down a bit."

"Genius," I laughed.

I had a sense my dad was deploying his anecdotes like smokebombs. In the end, I just gave up hoping that we would get on to something that mattered and surrendered to the party spirit.

"Where did you used to drink when you were in New York?" I asked, instead.

"We used to go El Morocco quite a bit," he reminisced, crossing one leg over the other and holding his champagne glass, rather grandly, on a level with his eyeline. It was getting dark outside now and I was really quite drunk.

"El Morocco?" I asked. "What's that?"

But Dad wasn't listening. He was off again: "I remember my friend who came from Beeville, Texas," he sighed. "He used to call me Chuck because I once leaned into, rather than out of, his Cadillac limo outside of El Morocco and was violently sick into it, rather than, as one more normally would be, onto the pavement."

He laughed at the memory, then added, "Sadly he was eventually taken away by the men in the white coats."

And so the night went on. Crazy stories and even crazier company. Somewhere along the line we gave in on the drinks as well and started drinking champagne too. Finally at 11pm the bar closed and Sasha and I got up to leave.

Dad still had more stories. "Did I tell you about the time I was staying with Claus and had to pretend to be Jewish?"

"No," I laughed.

"I got a crew cut and it revealed an unknown bald spot on my head. I had to buy a yarmulke on 7th Avenue to hide it."

Everyone was in hysterics. The Irishman was telling Sasha, "If you get in any trouble in New York, any trouble at all, call us, we can help. We know people in New York, OK?"

"See you later, cock," my dad was saying. "Send us a postcard."

As predicted, we had to abandon the bike and get a cab back home. We finished the packing in a drunken blur.

13

-581 DAYS

IN MOST NEW YORK stories the hero arrives in Manhattan with a suitcase and a dream. I pitched up with a suitcase and a hangover.

I had seven leaving parties in London, because my US working visa kept being delayed. I finally got it in May. The last party was at terminal three in Heathrow airport with Olly, who I had asked to be my best man at my wedding in September. As parties go, this one sucked. We sat and drank a couple of pints in a sterile pub in Departures until they called my flight.

"Well, I guess this is it," I said as I downed my Guinness.

"About time," said Olly.

"I mean it," I said, as I picked up my hand luggage, "I'm really going to cut down on my drinking in New York. And no coke."

"Yeah, right Tommy," scoffed Olly. Then he caught the fear in my face and softened, asking, "Do you mean it?"

I nodded furiously.

"Good luck mate," Olly said. "I'll come and see you soon."

We hugged, and I tried to think positive.

Being on airplanes always makes me emotional. I get sloppy and morose as I drink my way through the dislocation of the passing time zones, especially when I am alone. I thought of Sasha. Eighteen months earlier, Sasha had set up her own design business. Now, of course, it was beginning to take off. Little did I know that for the next two years we were going to spend almost half of our time apart as her business as an artist and designer would continually take her back and forth to Europe.

Really, I should stop drinking about now, I thought to myself as we flew over Sasha's house in Ireland and struck out for America, the Atlantic 40,000 feet below us. I imagined the plane blowing up, as I always do on planes, and tried to picture what it would be like to fall that far to your death. It would be okay if I was with Sasha. I would hold her as we went down and tell her I loved her all the way. But falling to my death with the guy in 45B for company? I hit the call button. "Vodka and tonic, please," I asked the stewardess. "Better make it a double."

Seven hours later I was somehow in a yellow New York cab bouncing down cobbled streets to my sister Alice's apartment. Alice was two years older than me and had moved to New York about two years earlier, following my sisters Lucy and Plum who both had high-profile jobs on glossy fashion magazines. Alice was doing well for herself in New York as well, and I wasn't too proud to be planning to blatantly hang on to the coat-tails of my sisters' success.

Alice lived in a giant loft apartment in the super-trendy Meatpacking district, with two English friends, Bridget – the girl who had introduced me to the features editor at the *Post* – and Claire.

Alice's apartment was above the cheapest supermarket in Manhattan. The only things we felt safe buying there were sealed goods like packets of rice and pasta or beers. Alice's room-mate, Claire, used to joke that the place, "smelt of Coke". It was true that the supermarket definitely had a bizarre odour and you had to try and not breathe through your nose too much when you were foraging for food or alcohol in there. The checkout queue took forever as the derelicts in front of you rifled through their pockets for money-back coupons and argued about the special offers.

But Alice's apartment was amazing. It was one huge, 1500 square-foot wood-floored room that had a kitchen at one end and a TV and sofas at the other with three box-rooms off the side. Alice had said that I could stay there until I found an apartment and Sasha arrived.

My "no-coke" rule lasted almost forty-eight hours. I arrived on the Thursday night, and by Saturday I was crushing a rock of cocaine under a $20 bill, scraping my credit card over the surface of the note until the drugs were milled into a fine powder. The stuff was half the price it was in England – about $50 a gramme – and, well, it just seemed churlish not to take advantage of the market. I chopped out a stubby line with my credit card, inhaled, and time just went *whum!*

At 5am that morning I was lying on Alice's sofa, desperately trying to get to sleep. Not a chance. The worry soundtrack was playing on a loop in my head, reminding me that I had to start work at the *New York Post* the next morning, that I was a stupid fuck and that I was going to be in big trouble if I couldn't keep away from the drugs.

Just about then the garbage trucks started. They beeped and crunched their way down 14th Street five floors down, occasionally pausing to empty huge containers of glass bottles. It sounded like an angry, alcoholic giant was doing his annual recycling trip on the corner of 9th Avenue.

Unfortunately the sound of crashing bottles didn't drown out the discussion raging in my head, endless remonstrations and recriminations, remorselessly cataloging how I had screwed up before I even began. I checked my watch. 5.30am. Christ. If I did get to sleep now, I wouldn't be able to sleep the next night. I would show up for work on my first day exhausted.

I heard a door open as Alice's room-mate Claire tiptoed to the bathroom.

"Hi Claire," I said to her as she made her way back.

"Tom," she said, starting, bleary eyed, "What are you still doing up?"

"I can't sleep," I said, sitting up on the sofa in my sleeping bag. "I feel like a big, toxic bag of shit. I am completely screwing this up and I don't know what to do. I promised myself I wouldn't take drugs out here, and well, here I am, on my second night, off my head on coke. I'm just sitting here worrying about how I am going to sleep tomorrow night, and that's keeping me awake now, and, oh shit, I don't know. I never should have come." A big tear rolled down my cheek.

Claire sat down on the end of my sofa and patted my knee through the sleeping bag. "You're just anxious," she said. "Really, really anxious. I could give you a Xanax if you want."

"What's Xanax?" I asked.

"It's an anti-anxiety," Claire said. "It just stops you freaking out about everything so you can get to sleep."

Anti-anxiety. That sounded good. I was just *anxious*. I looked at Claire. "Please," I said, surprised at the desperation in my voice.

Twenty minutes later I was gently floating away on a chemical sea of absolution. I pulled the sleeping bag up under my chin, self-consciously pulled a sleepy face for my own amusement and chuckled to myself. I could still hear the garbage trucks, but now, they were only coming through in waves. Like Pink Floyd, I giggled, I am comfortably numb. Another waterfall of glass reminded me I was in New York. I'd made it. And now, I was going to get some sleep.

-573 DAYS

i WOKE UP EARLY on Monday morning on Alice's sofa, showered in her tiny, dilapidated bathroom, shaved, put on my bespoke Kilgour suit, a freshly pressed pink shirt with silver cufflinks and a woven black silk tie dotted with spots of white. I checked myself in the mirror and clapped my hands, feeling satisfied. If there was one thing I could do, it was scrub up well. People forgive anything in a well-groomed man.

Bridget and I got the subway to work together. Bridget walked incredibly fast down 14th Street to the subway from the apartment, ducking and weaving through the solid side-walk crowd, glancing over her shoulder to check I was keeping up. It was like trying to follow a flying fish. The street was heaving. I had to turn sideways, suck in my stomach and flatten my arms by my side to weave past obese tourists from the Midwest, dart to the left and then right to find a way through the serried ranks of schoolkids walking four or five abreast and hop down into the road for half a pace or two just to keep Bridget in view.

It was only May, but it was hot that day, and when I got to the subway steps I was sweating. Bridget had beaten me by a minute and bought us both a bottle of water and a copy of the *Post*. We rattled up to 47th Street in about five minutes in an air-conditioned subway carriage. As a Londoner, I was used to spending at least forty minutes to go the same distance in London, usually in a hot, sweaty, smelly carriage where your nose invariably ended up in disgustingly close proximity to someone else's armpit. I mentioned my observations to Bridge. She smiled, and said, "It's not always like this. Before long you'll be bitching about the subway just as much as you did about the tube."

I love the first few days at a new job. You just sit around acquiring stationery, checking out the swivel on your chair and going for an endless round of lunches and coffees. No one expects anything. By Wednesday, when Faye sent me out on my first assignment, I had done little more than send emails to my friends back in the UK, put together a few basic story ideas and work out who was most likely to be at the boozer over the road, Langan's, after work (the answer I swiftly discovered was Steve Dunleavey, the *Post*'s resident drunk).

My first story was about a very rich, very annoying "Jewish American Princess" (JAP for short in New York slang) who had hired a stylist to help her clear out and organise her cavernous walk-in closets. When I got to the apartment the two of them were having a wild tug-of–war with a Gucci bag, surrounded by empty boxes from Fendi, Dior and Prada.

"Don't touch the fucking Gucci," the owner, a blonde bitch in her forties who had clearly had a lot of cosmetic surgery, was screaming, pulling the bag.

"You never fucking use it," the stylist, a skinny, twenty-something with black hair in a ponytail, boiling with ambition (she was the one who had called the *Post* to get coverage for the story) was yelling back, pulling the strap. "Just let it go!"

The battle was eventually settled by an expensive tearing noise. It went on like this all afternoon. After about four hours I couldn't bear it anymore and I headed back to the office and wrote it up. The resulting piece ran the next Monday over two pages ("Confessions of a Closet Monster"). My email crashed with all the congratulatory notes and pitches for other stories that rolled in from around the city.

I was on my way. For the first few months I usually wrote two or three big features a week, always focusing around the general areas of nightlife and going out or fashion and style. Thursday was the day the big "going out" section ran and I more or less ended up making it mine. I was a freelancer, but I was working five days a week, so I was making good money.

But my lifestyle of drinks, dinners and cocaine was expensive too. Luckily, when I did run short of cash I had a secret stash in my UK bank account – my £40,000 from the house. I would dip into my English bank account whenever I was running short, and if bill or bar tabs needed paying I would sometimes use my British Visa card, which was linked to the account.

Although technically I remained freelance, I became the chief nightlife writer for the *New York Post*. Every day my mailbox was a riot of brightly coloured envelopes containing invites to the night's events. Most were on thick card embossed with silver or red type, but if anyone went to the trouble of sending out slabs of lucite for their party then you knew it was going to be good. From the second week on, I was out every single night without fail, trying to get under the skin of the city's scene. Because I was still living with my sister and her girlfriends, I hung out and went out with them a lot. I joked that I was an honorary girl.

The very first thing I discovered was that, as far as these girls were concerned, New York has a chronic shortage of eligible single men. Everywhere I went high-earning, hard-bodied New York chicks would wander up to Alice and engage her in conversation. She would introduce me and the girls would talk animatedly to me for a little while.

"Oh, right, you are a writer at the *New York Post*, huh? Just moved here, yeah? Oh you're engaged! Oh wow congratulations! When's the wedding … oh, will you excuse me? I have to go … get a drink."

Being an eligible single guy in New York is like being a kid in a candy store. Being an engaged guy in New York with an absent wife is like being a diabetic kid in a candy store. You can look, but try to eat the goodies and you may seriously damage your health.

14

-563 DAYS

THE FIRST STEP to finding an apartment of my own in New York was to abandon all official channels. As I had not been issued with a social security number yet by the US government, had no credit record and was a freelance writer, real estate agents had taken to literally laughing me out of their open houses.

Instead, after three weeks of kipping on Alice's sofa I logged on to the website Craigslist and sublet a walk-up apartment in the East Village that was so small you could be in all three rooms at once and the bath was actually in a cupboard in the kitchen. I had to order an extra-small double bed which fitted into the tiny bedroom with just enough space on the sides to jam your hands down to tuck the sheet in. On one side the windows looked out onto brick walls that were literally 12 inches away.

I didn't really mind it being so small, and I thought the bath in the kitchen thing was kind of bohemian and cool.

Best of all, the place was only $1,200 a month – which meant that once Sasha got here it would be $600 each. It was next door to a tattoo parlour covered in mouldings of skulls, but, I reflected, you can't have it all, right?

I missed Sasha a lot. We were due to get married in September, but she was still stuck in Ireland for most of that first summer, trying to finish off the redesign of a hotel bar in Dublin that wasn't working out well and kept delaying her. It rained every single weekend for twelve weeks – big, sweaty, tropical downpours, while at home, they were having one of the finest summers on record.

Without Sasha to go out drinking with I had lost my partner in crime. We'd speak every day on the phone, and I would tell her which parties I had been to the night before, discuss the intensity of my hangover, and count the days till she was due to arrive in New York.

Still, I wasn't entirely alone – my building, I soon discovered, was swarming with cockroaches, mice and other unappetising life forms. When I came back to the apartment late at night and switched the light on, there would be an explosion of insect activity around the sink, as dozens of albino earwigs that looked like something out of *Alien* dived for the homely darkness of the drain.

Sasha was able to come over for about two weeks either side of my twenty-ninth birthday in June. I was so proud of finding the apartment, but Sasha's face fell when she walked in from her cab. It stank of weed – I had found a dealer by this stage who, in true New York style, delivered – and the fridge contained nothing but beer. I showed her the bath in the cupboard in the kitchen and she did her best to laugh.

Then she said, "Monk, I'm knackered after the flight. I'm going to get an early night."

"What? You're going to bed? Don't you want to go out for a drink?" I asked. "It's your first night in New York?"

The panic in my voice panicked me.

"Exactly," said Sasha, nuzzling up to me. "I want to get into bed with my Monk."

"Oh, okay," I said. "Do you want a beer first?" I broke away from her and reached into the fridge to get one for her.

"No Monk," said Sasha, impatiently now. "I want to get into bed. I'm exhausted from the flight and I haven't seen you for almost two months."

She walked three paces to the tiny bedroom.

"OK," I said. "I'll be right through."

I sat on the sofa and finished my beer. Then I rolled up a joint. Then I thought, what the hell, and got another beer from the fridge. It was early. I drank another beer, and another, until, quite suddenly, it was late, and the fridge was empty. But I wasn't tired. Sasha was asleep. I couldn't *believe* she hadn't wanted to go out. Was this what marriage was going to be like? Boring? Surely she wouldn't notice if I nipped out for a drink.

I tiptoed silently to the door. The wood creaked. Sasha heard.

"Monk?" she said from the bedroom. "Where are you going?"

"I'm just popping out to get something," I said, "I'll be right back."

And I went. I headed straight to Karma, on 2nd Avenue, one of the last bars in New York City where you could legally smoke, and drank bourbon until they closed at 4am.

I sat at the bar, trying to ignore a drunk taxi driver who wanted to talk, thinking "You can't be doing this"; thinking "Your fiancée's just got back are you insane?" and then thinking, "Well, you may as well have one more shot to help you sleep."

I kept thinking I'd leave after the next drink, but for some reason I couldn't, or wouldn't.

You must go home to your fiancée now. You must go home now, she just got in. Ah, fuck it, give me one more Jack and Coke for the road.

-556 DAYS

THE NEXT MORNING I woke up on the sofa in the sitting room, late and ashamed and horribly hungover. I peeked into the bedroom. Sasha wasn't there. I ran one of my hot baths and smoked a joint while I was in there scalding and sweating myself better. When Sasha finally came back an hour or so later I was starting to get wrinkly from the water.

"Hi gorgeous," I said as she came in.

She wouldn't look at me. She was stuffing groceries into the fridge.

"Babes, I don't think you have to put sugar in the fridge."

She turned to face me and her eyes were all puffy from where she had been crying. I didn't know what to say. So I said the stupidest thing ever. I said, "Are you pissed off with me because of last night?"

"I'm not pissed off, I'm upset," Sasha sobbed back. "I'm giving up a lot to be here, Tom. And we're supposed to be getting married in four months and you would rather spend the night in a bar than with me when I've just got here?"

"I'm sorry," I said. "I just needed a drink to get to sleep. It won't happen again."

"Well, I don't care," said Sasha. She sat down on the tiny chair at the tiny kitchen table and looked around the tiny apartment and swallowed. She looked at me hard and said, "Maybe there is something wrong if you have to go and drink like that."

"What do you mean? Do you think I should stop?"

There was silence for a few seconds. "I'm not going to nag you about your drinking Tom," she said. "If you want to drink go ahead and drink. I'm not going to become some nagging wife."

I was shocked. "But Monk if you think I am drinking too much please tell me."

Sasha sighed. "Tom, of course you are drinking too much if you are going out until five in the morning when you haven't see your wife for three weeks and then sleeping on the sofa. I think you should cut down. But I don't see why I should have to be the one who becomes a nag."

"What do you mean?" I asked, genuinely baffled. If she wanted me to stop drinking, all she had to do was say the word.

"Look, Tom," she said, "We both like going out and getting wasted. That's what a lot of our relationship is based on. We got drunk the first time we met, remember?"

I nodded. Were we really just about getting drunk together?

Sasha carried on, "In Ireland, everybody drinks! All my friends and family drink. So of course I don't want you to stop drinking and become some boring person who never does anything."

"No, of course not," I said, heaving a sigh of relief. Thank God I didn't have to stop drinking after all.

"But the great thing about you, about us, is that we have always been able to hold it together no matter how fucked we get. I like that about you. But last night wasn't funny. It was just ... weird."

Silence.

"OK," I said, suddenly ashamed and frightened again, worried she was about to leave me, looking for the magic words that could make everything all right.

I held my nose and submerged my head under the water for a few seconds. What could I say? How could I hold it together?

I burst up into the air again, exhaling.

"I'll cut down," I said, "Really, I will. Everything's going to be fine. You want to go and get some breakfast?"

15

-547 DAYS

M Y ARRIVAL in New York coincided with another notable British import, a swanky private members club called Soho House, conveniently located right across the street from Alice's apartment.

Working on the tried-and-tested premise that people – and New Yorkers especially – always want what they can't get, Soho House had become insanely popular because the club would hardly let anyone join. It had less than a thousand members in the first few months, all of whom had to pay an annual subscription of $1,000. A disproportionately large proportion of those thousand individuals had been invited to join by my absurdly social brother-in-law Euan, who was on the membership committee for the club.

Euan was married to Lucy, Plum's twin sister, and although I was not a member of Soho House (I couldn't spare the thousand bucks) I could usually get past the dopey door staff at ground level by dropping Euan's name at the door. Then you would go through to the back of lobby, step into the leather-padded elevators and be whisked up to the sixth floor of the building, which was decorated in rich, masculine leather and wood. The seating area was dominated by huge armchairs and sofas with supermodels and actresses artfully sprawled over them.

If Euan wasn't there, which was unlikely in the first few months of the club's existence, one of my sisters or one of my British friends was likely to be there and I would just discreetly look at the log book on the front desk, where members had to sign in, and say their names instead. It all meant that Soho House quickly became my default hangout spot in the first few months.

The bar at Soho House was expensive, but not much more so than any other trendy bar in New York. A cocktail was about twelve dollars, a bottle of champagne less than a hundred. The expense was easily justified by the parade of stars that flowed in. Ethan Hawke, Uma Thurman and Gwen Stefani would all hang out there in a startlingly low-key way. I always got more excited by the British celebs who would show up: David Bowie, Eddie Izzard and on one memorable occasion David Beckham and his wife Victoria, who were attending a party thrown by *Vogue* editor Anna Wintour.

So everything was going according to plan in August 2003. I had been in New York for about three months, and I was writing the going out pages every Thursday. It was a great job for discovering the city. I wrote about the best cocktails in town, which of the new, hot restaurants and hotels had the best bar scene and which clubs were best for rubbing shoulders with models and celebrities. The only thing I was forbidden from writing about was Soho House, which had a strict "no press" rule. I started to get messages from restaurant publicists inviting me to check out the new venues they were promoting, promising they would "take care" of the check.

I told Euan about these solicitations. "Nice one," he said. "T F R."

"T F R?" I asked quizzically.

"Yeah baby," said Euan, "Total Free Ride!"

-520 DAYS

THE ONLY PROBLEM was that I had been on a monstrous bender ever since I arrived. All my good intentions to cut down on alcohol and drugs had come to nothing. It was a case of New York, same old me.

Or, possibly, even worse me. In London a shot of alcohol is a carefully measured 25ml. In New York, they keep pouring vodka into your glass until you say stop. In London the bars close at 11pm. In New York even the average neighbourhood pub was open till 4am. And in London I had to pay for my drinks. In New York, thanks to my job writing nightlife features for the *Post*, people couldn't give me enough free booze.

The killer, though, was that having promised Olly I would stay away from drugs, I was doing more cocaine than ever. Coke was cheap and pure compared to what I had been used to in London, and the drug seemed to go well with New York's frenetic pace. And everyone else was doing it. It felt normal and so did I.

But a few familiar problems were starting to recur. I kept getting to work later and later in the morning because I would oversleep. I always seemed to be broke, waking up with a pocket full of crumpled receipts and a few single dollar bills, despite the fact I was earning good money at the *Post*. I withdrew cash from my English bank account, the house sale money, more and more regularly. It was soon down to about £25,000. I would feel a rush of guilt and panic, washing like a wave of shame from my toes to the tip of my head whenever I thought about how I was frittering away my inheritance, but I told myself that there had been a lot of expenses involved in setting up our new life in New York.

The latest of these expenses was moving out of the East Village. Sasha had found a much more spacious one-bedroom apartment on 55th Street in midtown Manhattan. It was a splendid, cockroach-free place, with plenty of natural light and wooden floors. It was reasonably cheap because it was a fourth floor walk-up and it was in an unfashionable part of midtown, but I came to love everything about our block, from the Robert Indiana LOVE statue on the corner of 55th and 6th to the pub where they would let you smoke after midnight, to the amazing French restaurant opposite us called La Bonne Soupe where we swiftly befriended the owner, Yves, and the manager, Jean. Whenever Sasha was away, taking care of her business back in Ireland or London, I would live almost exclusively on their famed onion soup.

But the drinking was crazy. After I slept in till 2pm and missed an 11am appointment with a men's clothing designer who was going to let me walk the catwalk in his show during fashion week for a story, I decided to try to quit drinking for a week to prove I wasn't an alcoholic. I got good and drunk on the Sunday night, ordered $100 worth of pot, and smoked huge quantities of weed every night before going to the cinema for the rest of the week. I managed to get to Friday night without drinking.

That Friday I went to join Euan and a few other friends for dinner at Soho House. We sat down to eat, and I decided that, not having had a drink *all week* (well, since Sunday, anyway), just one glass of wine with dinner couldn't hurt. The waitress came over to take our order. The other guys at the table ordered a bottle of wine, and when the waitress turned to me I ordered a steak, and asked, "Also, I would like a glass of Merlot. But could you please bring it to me with my main course?" She nodded, went away, and returned immediately with my wine, which she placed on the table in front of me, and scooted off back to the kitchen before I could protest.

I was furious. Now I had to sit here all through the appetisers with this glass of wine in front of me, and not drink it if I wanted to have a glass of wine with my steak. I waved at the waitress again, who came hurrying over.

"Hi how can I help?" she asked.

"Yeah, the thing is, I ordered this glass of wine to come with my main course," I said, "But they brought it right away. Could you take it away and bring it with my main course please?"

The waitress looked at me peevishly and gave her eyes a quarter roll. It was a busy Friday night. "Why don't you just keep that glass of wine and drink it when your main course comes?" she suggested patronisingly.

"Because," I snapped, "I only want to drink one glass of wine and if you leave this here then I'll drink it now."

Too late, I realised what I had said and how I had said it. The air at the table changed. The temperature dropped a couple of degrees, and then it got very warm. My brother-in-law and his friends stopped talking and looked at me. So did the waitress. She picked up the glass of wine and marched off with it to the kitchen, shouting, "Cancel the glass of wine," at the top of her voice. Bitch, I thought to myself.

Eventually it was time for the main course. The waitress came over with our plates. I tried to be ingratiating. "Could I please have that glass of wine back?" I asked.

She looked at me in utter disbelief. "You want a glass of wine now?"

"Yes, please," I said. "That's what I said in the beginning. I asked for a glass of wine with my main course."

"Are you sure about that?"

Bitch.

The waitress brought the wine back to my table.

"Thank you," I said, dismissing her, my voice saying, "This is *her* fault."

I drank the glass as slowly as I could with my steak. It tasted so good. The – admittedly foreshortened – week of abstinence had been worth it. I could taste the wine's hundreds of different flavours exploding around my tongue. The slight smokiness. The tannic bite. The *alcohol.*

God it was good. It was so good, in fact, that I went up to the roof deck right afterwards and drank six margaritas to celebrate the success of my little experiment.

16

-489 DAYS

I ORGANISED A GIANT T F R when Euan and my sister Lucy had their baby boy Heathcliff. Lucy didn't want to come out, and Sasha was still in Ireland, preparing for our wedding, so I made it an all-boy affair. I rang up one of my best restaurant-owning friends, Jean-Luc, who had a sleek bistro on the Upper West Side which I had written about recently, and asked if he would throw dinner for us.

"Tommy Sykes!" he said, when I identified myself. "Of course you can come here for dinner! How many are you?"

"About twelve," I said.

I'm told it was a night to remember. We started off at JL, where we worked our way through cocktails, wine and dinner. We left a tip for the staff, but the bill – which must have topped $1,000 – was taken care of by Jean-Luc. Next stop was the Penthouse Executive Club, a strip joint on the West Side, where I had called up ahead to get us all free entry. It was depressing and sleazy in the way that strip clubs always are. The idea always sounds great but the harsh reality of some desperate East European girl shaking her arse in your face tends to be somewhat less thrilling. We didn't hang around long. We wanted to get to Soho House. The club was at the very apex of its cool.

This is how I remember it: I was standing by the bar, ordering drinks at first. I was drinking big, New York buckets of martini, feeling very drunk. Then we were standing in a circle in the middle of the room. It was very late, and we were the only people left there. One of our group – in fact, a fairly senior guy in the publishing world – pulled out a joint and lit it.

Most of my memories of things that happen to me when I am in a drink or drug blackout are just fragments. This time, I can remember seeing my leather shoes outlined on the tessellated wooden floor of the bar, two olives parked one above the other in the empty glass on the bar and my friend pulling out the joint. Then I saw the flare of the lighter as he lit it, him smiling and laughing, and me holding the joint between my thumb and two first fingers, taking a deep draw.

In retrospect, it's easy to say that lighting up a joint anywhere in public was clearly not a smart move. The smoking of *cigarettes* had been banned in New York just three months before, so there wasn't even any tobacco smoke to cover the smell of the weed. The next thing I remember a lot of people were shouting and I was saying,

"All right, all right! Just don't touch me, OK? Don't fucking touch me!"

I refused to leave the bar. It was past two in the morning but I wouldn't be moved. I demanded they go and get the manager, Podge, out of bed from his apartment three blocks away to throw me out in person.

-488 DAYS

I WOKE UP LATE for work the next morning, and called Euan on my way down 6th Avenue to the offices of the *Post*.

"Hey man, great night last night," I said when he answered.

Silence. Then, "Do you remember what you did last night Tom?" he asked me.

"Erm, yeah. We went to JL, then that strip club, then Soho House…"

I took a sip of Gatorade. Something had happened. I sighed and gave up, "No. I can't remember man. What *did* I do last night?"

He told me.

"Oh, shit," I said.

I called Podge to apologise but I was banned from the club. Euan put in a special word for me, and the owner of the club, Nick Jones, agreed to ban me for three months, after which time I would be allowed back in as long as I had a family member to vouch for me. It reminded me of the time I was rusticated at school. By the time I quit drinking, I had been banned a record-breaking three times from Soho House.

Just before I was due to get married, in September 2003, the gossip pages of the *New York Observer* got hold of the story. I was terrified that if they ran an item about how I had been smoking pot in public the *Post* would fire me. What a wedding present that would be.

It reminded me of what my friend and fellow party animal Godfrey Deeney had told me a few months before when we were drinking late one night. "You're a good lad Tom and New York loves you at the moment," he said, "But if you screw up, and you get caught screwing up, they'll drop you so fucking fast you won't even see the sidewalk before you hit it."

I was about to be dropped. I could see the pavement rising to meet me.

I decided my best hope for the *New York Observer* was to obfuscate. I admitted to the reporter who eventually called me that I had been banned for smoking – but I denied it was pot. I tried to make a self-effacing joke about how the Brits were bad tippers and hoped they would run that instead.

I ran out of the house to pick up the paper the following Monday.

*At **Soho House**, the Brit-packed private club in the meatpacking district, the **Sykes** name is something of a* *mainstay.* Marie Claire *editor at large* **Lucy Sykes** *is a member, as are her sisters* **Plum** *and* **Alice**. *But it looks like brother* **Tom** *has been banned. According to* **Soho House** *committee member Tim Geary, Mr.* **Sykes** *has been banned "because he's not a member" but frequently attempted to gain entrance to the club as if he were.*

Though Mr. **Sykes** *confirmed that he is not a member of the club, he disputed some of the finer points of Mr. Geary's statement. Mr.* **Sykes** *said he was banned for three months in the summer, but has since been allowed to cross the threshold once more as a guest of his family members. "I was basically asked to stay away for a couple of months during the summer because I was smoking" – Mayor Bloomberg's smoking ban extends to private clubs – "and being obstreperous, and in true Brit fashion, I think, I wasn't tipping enough, but I've only got my Britishness to blame," Mr.* **Sykes** *said. "I completely understand and I put my hands up to it."*

I laughed and laughed and laughed. I was standing on the corner of 55th and 6th and I had to sit down on the black metal base LOVE statue because I was laughing so hard. I laughed harder than the crack addicts who used to congregate there late at night did when they had been smoking their stuff.

Everything was working out fine. A few days later Sasha and I flew to Ireland, where we were married.

17

-495 DAYS

I USED TO HATE Wednesdays because at my primary school they made us do country dancing on a Wednesday. We had to line up and prance around the sports hall to the tune of *The Flying Scotsman*. At Eton, Wednesday was the day when you were supposed to do Cadet Corps – basically pretend to be in the army and develop the skills and mindset necessary for a career spent killing poor people in hot places.

All that changed when I got to New York though. Now, I hated Tuesdays. Every Tuesday there was a features meeting on the tenth floor offices of the *Post* at 10am. It was the earliest I ever got to the office. Usually I wouldn't show till midday. Well, I was the nightlife writer, so surely it was only natural that I should be a late-to-bed, late-to-rise kind of guy, right? Being late was part of my *job*.

But Tuesdays were the one day a week where I couldn't be late. The meetings always filled me with dread. The features editor, Faye, sat at the end of a long table in one of the conference rooms, and the reporters sat around the edge. It looked like a dinner party but if you didn't have any ideas it felt just like a firing squad.

On Monday nights I would be gripped with fear and start scribbling down ideas in my notebook. The long lists paid testament to my toxic lifestyle and melted brain. "Sake – is it hot?"; "Caipirinhia – the new mojito?" and "Hangover cures – a road test".

Whenever I was really stuck, I'd propose a classic stunt, where I would get dressed up, get photographed doing something outrageous and then write eight hundred funny words about it. I loved doing stunts. In the UK I had been known for them ever since the tights photo gave me my first brush with notoriety. I had dyed my hair blond ("Do blonds really have more fun? Our man with the peroxide finds out!") and ridden a horse named Diesel around London to "beat the fuel strike" when lorry drivers blockaded the country's refineries in protest at fuel prices. My friend Tom Newton-Dunne, who worked at the *Daily Mirror*, did the ultimate stunt when he was photographed playing pool in the nude with a crazy guy who kept getting arrested for attempting to walk the length of Britain naked. He was made the defence correspondent at the *Mirror*. Tom, that is, not the naked hill walker.

In New York I started out small. I smuggled a dog into the cinema in Times Square ("Pup quiz – Where can you really take a dog in NYC?"), then devoted several nights to lighting up cigarettes in bars in an effort to demonstrate that the smoking ban was being widely flouted ("This way to the Smoke-easy!").

Stunts were embarrassing but readers loved them. And I was never in any doubt about the strength of my egotism. I adored seeing my face plastered all over the front page of the features section. It was always a thrill – even if I was wearing lingerie. My email would ping reassuringly all day with congratulatory messages from publicists and less-good-natured insults from my friends for stripping myself of any remaining dignity in pursuit of a byline.

What I really wanted though, was a regular column. A column that fitted around my heavy-drinking, hard-partying lifestyle, which I could get paid to write every week. So one Tuesday morning, I suggested we needed a new bar column.

"What's the idea?" asked Faye.

"Well, I figure there's two ways of looking at the New York scene," I said. "Either you can do a massive bird's eye view of the whole thing – you know, '100 reasons why New York is still the best city in the world' – or you go totally, totally micro and put a tiny area under the microscope. Like, 'What's happening on the corner of 12th Street and 3rd Avenue?'"

Faye looked interested for a moment. Faye was a tough editor and if she didn't like your idea she let you know fast, usually using the word "sucks".

"I like the neighbourhood idea," she said to me, then to

her deputy, "Didn't we have a plan for something like this once? Wasn't it called *Block Party*?"

"That's a *great* name," I said, pressing, my heart beating harder than the barman at the Passerby Bar – a favourite spot with a flashing floor straight out of *Saturday Night Fever* on 15th Street – shook my martinis.

"Let's call it *Block Party*," I continued, on a roll now. "Each week, I can write about all the bars and the nightlife character of a different block. People want local right now."

Faye hesitated for a fiftieth of a second. *She's going to call me on it*, I thought. *She knows it's just an excuse to get wasted on their dime.*

Instead I heard Faye say, "OK, let's do it." Then she switched her attention to someone else in the room. "Farrah, what you got?"

Farrah started talking about her ideas, but it was all white noise. A little man in my head was shaking a bottle of champagne and popping the cork in an explosion of cheers and bubbles.

I called Sasha to tell her the news the moment I got out of the meeting.

"Where will we start?" she asked.

"I don't know. Anywhere. There must be a million bars in New York. A thousand blocks to choose from. This one will run and run."

-350 DAYS

OVER THE NEXT YEAR, I wrote around fifty *Block Party* columns. If I thought I had the greatest job in the world before, now I really did. *I was the bar columnist for the New York Post*. My drinking problem was no longer a liability. It was a qualification, a vocation, a career. All my life had been leading up to this.

I was paid $300 for each column, but that wasn't the lure of *Block Party*. Sure, three hundred bucks a week helped pay the rent, but, more importantly, as the column began to get a following, I was besieged by restaurant publicists inviting me to go and eat for free at their fancy establishments and put them in the column.

Thus began in earnest the year of freebie living. I would get to the office by midday, and sit at my piled-high, chaotic desk, listening to my voicemail and deleting everything in my email that wasn't porn or a potentially interesting drinking opportunity. The publicists obviously couldn't say anything as blatant as, "We'll give you a free five-course dinner and all the wine you and your wife can drink if you write about us." They used code words instead. They would say, "Let me know when we can set that up for you", "We'll take care of you", or, my personal favourite, "Just take care of the staff", which meant, "Please leave a healthy tip".

Sasha and I lived a bizarre double life. We would have to scratch around behind the sofa to try and find enough quarters to get eggs for breakfast, but by 9pm we would be eating a $50 egg for a starter at dinner. I'm thinking of one egg in particular here, at the uptown restaurant davidburke & donatella. The egg had been painstakingly hollowed out, the top cut off in a perfect Humpty Dumpty crown, the shell had then been filled with a delicious onion flan mixture which had been poured back into the egg, baked, and lovingly topped with caviar.

After work I would either go to the pub or head home to change, and then Sasha and I would take the subway to the stop nearest the restaurant to save on cab fares. We would announce ourselves to the host at the Biltmore Room, The Strip House or Lever House, and the show would begin.

First up was usually the general manager, who would show us to our table, while I asked some well-practised questions to cement my status as a VIP journalist it would be in their interests to give special treatment to. How long had they been open? ("About a month, now, and we have been packed every night.") What was the culinary focus of the kitchen? ("Italian, sir. The chef is famous for the calf cheek fettucine.") Oh, and did they have an extensive wine list? ("We have over two thousand bottles, sir, with a focus on the great vintages of the Languedoc region.")

Once we were seated at our table, gleaming with more glassware and cutlery than we used at home in a week, the just-French-enough head waiter or maitre d' would appear. He would talk us through the menu and then tell us he would give us a few minutes to think about our order. In the meantime, would we like a cocktail or some wine?

At this moment Sasha and I would look at each other, and raise our eyebrows as if to say, "Well, shall we? I mean, we don't usually, but *shall* we, just this once?"

The cocktails would arrive, and the waiter would ask if we knew what we would like to eat.

"No," I would reply, setting aside the menu with an air of defeat. "We'd like to ask a favour. Could you please just choose for us? This menu looks so fabulous, and we don't want to miss anything. We want to try whatever the chef thinks is the very best on the menu."

The waiter would smile, flattered. "Certainly sir. And for the wine?"

"Is there a sommelier?" I would inquire. "This wine list looks so fabulous, and we really don't want to miss anything there either…"

Once the waiter had left our table Sasha and I would grin at each other. Was this really happening?

-203 DAYS

WEEK AFTER WEEK – sometimes several times a week in fact – I inhaled deeply at the intoxicating trough of New York restaurant publicity. Five-course dinners with three bottles of wine, preceded by cocktails and suffixed by brandies, became the norm. I became bolder, ordering $100, $150 bottles of wine. On one occasion I asked the sommelier to bring me the best Italian wine he had. He actually did it as well. I began to say I needed a table for four or *six* people and Sasha and I would bring friends, or my sisters and their husbands and boyfriends. It was absolutely outrageous.

The tips alone became a major financial burden. On a thousand dollar dinner, you really have to tip $250 in New York. If it was $250 I didn't have, so what. I would put it on my credit card – linked to my house sale money – and forget about it.

I guess the only difference between me and Sasha was that I was never ready to go home after dinner. Sometimes Sasha would say she had had enough for one night. Couldn't we go home?

I would get into a mood. Didn't she understand? I couldn't write a column about just one restaurant. I had to check out the other bars on the block. It was my *job*. The column was called *Block Party*. Not, well, *Expensive Restaurant* – although, that wasn't a bad idea, actually.

So on we would go, into the night, into the party, me leading the way, Sasha following, maybe with a few other friends we had taken for dinner, a merry little band of drunks. Into every bar on the block we would go. "We'll just check their martinis," I would say. "Research."

One of my favourite areas in the city was the strip of hip bars starting at the corner of 1st and 1st, and one week I decided to cover the block for the column. We started off with dinner and cocktails at a Moroccan place called Chez es Saada. It was about 10pm by the time we finished dinner, and I wanted a cigarette. That smoking had been banned didn't stop me. I lit one up, hiding the cigarette under the table. Sasha looked at me disapprovingly. "Tommy," she said. "Don't smoke in here. It's really rude. They've just given us an amazing dinner."

"They don't mind," I said, and called over a waiter and ordered another cocktail – a Steve McQueen (Maker's Mark, blackberry nectar and fresh lemon juice) – to make the point. The waiter said nothing about the smoke rising from under the table. He knew I was from the *Post*, I thought. He wouldn't *dare*.

By 11pm we were ready for the next stop on our journey. There were two bars almost next to each other on the block, Starfoods and the Elephant, and we spent the rest of the night bouncing between the two of them.

Our English friend Anna-Louise was in Starfoods with a bunch of her mates, so we spent most of the rest of the night there. I let the manager know, through Anna, who I was, and the drinks flowed freely.

The last thing I remember I was on the dance floor with Anna and she was shouting something into my ear. Some guy was a bastard.

"Who?"

"The manager at Elephant," she said. "He's a bastard. I was seeing him. He said he would pick me up in his car the other day and left me on the motorway for three hours."

"What?" I said. "Why?"

"Because he's a bastard. Can you put the fact that he's a bastard in your column?"

I laughed. "Er, I dunno Anna."

"Oh please please please," she said. "Please!"

She really was a lovely girl. "Well, OK, I'll try," I said.

-202 DAYS

dAYLIGHT. Where am I? No Sasha, she must have gone out already. Why am I still wearing all my clothes from last night? Why am I on the sofa not in my bed? I notice a half-burnt joint that must have been unravelling all night, spilling burnt marijuana and tobacco all over my white shirt. I must have tried to smoke it last night. It's almost 80% weed. That's lucky, I think, guessing that's why it went out rather than burning down the house – or a hole in my leg.

My head throbs violently. My mouth tastes of alcohol – stale whiskey and sambuca. What did I do last night? I dig into my pockets. They are stuffed full of mashed-up receipts with crazy signatures and single dollar bills, but there is also a small notebook in there. I pull it out and look at it with interest.

It's my notes for the evening. They say, "Chez es Saada, Moroccan. Steve McQueen. Elephant, Thai – cool. Starfoods – hipster crowd. Dancing. Manager of Elephant bastard says Anna. Mars Bar. Home 4am."

I look at the notebook like an archaeologist examining evidence of an ancient civilisation. Believe it or not, this actually qualifies as pretty detailed notes for *Block Party*. It's lucky I have them because I can't remember a thing. I look at the scribble again. I actually went to the Mars Bar after all that? The Mars Bar is a major, major dive, with broken chairs, layers of solid graffiti on the wall and filthy toilets, on the corner of 1st and 2nd. It's one of my favourite bars.

I start unfolding the receipts on my bed, counting the bills that remain. Somehow I have spent over $200 during the course of last night. I feel sick at the realisation. It doesn't make any sense. Dinner was free, after all, and so were the drinks in Starfoods. How the hell did I get through $200? I look in my wallet again, just to check, and I see an empty bag of cocaine.

Oh, yeah. I remember now. Someone ordered some coke and I ended up paying for it. $50 or whatever. I groan and lie back on my bed. I check the clock. 11.34. Not too bad, I suppose. I can make it in by 12.30. I suffer for my art.

FIRST THINGS FIRST
Block Party by Tom Sykes

The easiest thing about getting to this part of town is the cab ride there – all you have to say is First and First. The hardest thing is leaving: Block Party didn't make it home until 4am – and that was a school night.

Kick off at the Moroccan-themed basement of Chez
es Saada with dinner and a "Steve McQueen" cocktail
and admire the elegant crowd, then head for Elephant,
a Thai joint with a great bar and an infectious beat.
Don't get too cosy with the staff though. Sources told
Block Party the manager's a heartbreaker. (He didn't
return calls by press time.)

The editor responsible for overseeing the column sent me
an email the next day. "Love the column on First and First.
It's great."

I leaned back on my chair and cracked my fingers.
Today's hangover was subsiding. I loved this town. I could
not believe how great my job was. I loved *Block Party*. At
last, I had done it. I really was getting paid to go out and
get wasted.

My head hurt most mornings and my bank account was
a disaster zone, but I was living an incredible life. Free
dinners, drinking in every bar around town – and now publicists were even sending bottles of liquor to my office in an
effort to get me to write about them. I was the party, alcohol and nightlife correspondent at the *New York Post*. Result.

There were a few minor issues though, which I
preferred not to think about. I was drunk every night. Sasha
had decided that the problem was drinking whiskey, which
she claimed brought on "the whiskey madness", so I had
been banned from drinking that anymore. My heart hurt
and palpitated with alarming frequency from all the coke I

was doing and weed I was smoking. I hadn't had sex for days – or was that weeks – because I was always too wasted at night, and Sasha would be gone in the morning. I felt ashamed every time I got money out of my house account, which now had less than £10,000 left in it. But I couldn't expense the cocaine, or the $100 restaurant tips, could I? I was too clever to put in $200 worth of receipts for *Block Party*. $40 maybe – you know, a drink in every bar. That's what a normal person would have. Not six drinks in every bar. I didn't want to give the game away. The bar owners knew I was into getting wasted and high, but I didn't want to give my editors at the *Post* reason to suspect it. I didn't want to blow my cover. Not now, when everything was going so well. I didn't want to think about all that shit. I wanted to think about tonight. I wanted to go out.

I called a publicist.

"Hi, it's me."

"Hi Tom. What can we do for you?"

"Can you set me up for dinner for four tonight please?"

I hung up and flipped through my Rolodex, wondering which of my mates would be game for a spot of "research" tonight.

18

-150 DAYS

IN JULY 2004, midway through my second year at the *Post*, Ian Spiegelman, one of the regular contributors to the *New York Post*'s gossip column, *Page Six*, was sacked. One drunken night he had fired off an email to Doug Dechert, who Spiegelman believed to be a double-crossing source. He threatened, among other things, to "push [his] face inside out in private or public" and referred to him as an, "ageing trust-fund pussy". Proving that drunken typing can be every bit as dangerous as drunken driving, Dechert immediately forwarded the email on to our rivals at the *New York Daily News*, and Spiegelman was toast by breakfast.

I had worked a few shifts on *Page Six* covering for staff vacations, so when Ian was fired I was given a regular shift on the column every Friday. *Page Six* runs every day of the week in the *New York Post* (although, through an accident of history, the column is never actually found on page six of the newspaper) and it is undoubtedly the most powerful bit of print real estate in the city. Everyone in New York who counts reads *Page Six* every day, so anyone who has anything to promote is desperate to get a mention in the column, and there were items every day about who had been seen doing what to whom the night before, and every club or bar owner wanted to make sure it was their establishment's name that got attached to the boldfaced names we mentioned.

Page Six was really three people. There was the editor, the unflappable, deadpan Richard Johnson, and his two deputies, the feisty, fast-talking and foul-mouthed Paula Froelich and the whip-smart and charming Chris Wilson. Being the bar columnist for the *New York Post* had given me the keys to the city, but being the bar columnist who also had a regular gig on *Page Six* was like getting a special bunch personalised with my name picked out in diamonds and gold.

It also gave me another partner in crime. Chris had become my best friend since I had been in New York. First and foremost this was because Chris was always up for going out and drinking until the early hours of the morning. I only had to get up for work one day a week (Fridays had taken the place of Tuesdays as my new least favourite day), but Chris had to be in the office every day at 10.30 Monday through Friday. 10.30 doesn't sound very early, but when you're out till 4am it's plenty early enough. Chris was late for work more often than not, but he would often stay later in the evening than Paula and help put the page to bed so it all seemed to balance out. And a column like *Page Six* had to have someone out there walking the walk of the world that the page talked about.

Chris was the single greatest person to go out partying with in New York City. He knew all the nightlife characters, and no matter which club or bar we pitched up outside, the bouncers and bar staff would welcome Chris (and me, and anyone else who happened to be with him) in with open arms. Chris was outrageous, hilarious, charming and never gave a damn what anyone thought or said about him. And, unlike Sasha, Chris was always up for going out as hard and as late as, if not later than me.

Chris and I were a team. He believed, as I did, that getting drunk and partying all night made you a more effective chronicler of the nightlife scene. He understood that drinking was an essential part of the job. One day we'd change – just not right now.

"You couldn't do this job if you were sober," Chris told me at four one morning as we sat in his apartment polishing off the night with a six-pack of beer and listening to Black Flag. "There is so much at your disposal as a reporter on *Page Six*," he said. "I mean, think about it. There are two or three events every night, private parties where you not only have a full entrée, but you get your ass totally kissed. You never wait in line, you never pay for a drink. You don't have to deal with all that bullshit around the clubs. We have superhuman nightlife powers."

I spent more and more time hanging out with Chris. We ran into Bridget one day when we were leaving work to go to the pub across the street, Langans, and she said, "Oh my God – it's the terrible twins." The terrible twins, I liked that.

Chris was one of the few people I had ever met who drank his beers at the same speed as me. Usually when I was with a group of people and I finished my beer and said, "Right, who wants another?", everyone would say, "I'm OK," or "I'm still working on this one." But with Chris when we got to Langans, it was like, "Beer?"

"Yup."

"Beer?"

Chug-a-lug-lug.

"Sure, why not?"

Work was on 47th Street and Chris lived on 49th. After a few drinks at the pub we would sometimes head back to his place for a joint to keep the ball rolling.

If there was one area where Chris disappointed me, it was his appetite for weed. I could (and frequently did) smoke weed all day and all night, but after a puff or two Chris would hand the joint back to me, and decline to smoke anymore. "I'm gonna be wiped out," he'd say. "How can you smoke so much of that stuff?"

I didn't really know the answer. I would buy ounce bags of marijuana for about $100, and just smoke and smoke and smoke until it was gone. Usually, after the first or second joint I would start to feel weak, tongue-tied or paranoid, but that never stopped me. I would just think that another one might make me feel better. I was like one of those people who can't stop washing their hands, except I couldn't stop smoking pot. More times than I can remember I would flush all my marijuana down the toilet, only to find myself frantically calling my dealer a few hours later to arrange another delivery. I would catch myself for a moment and think, *This is insane*, but it made no difference. I just wanted to have one more hit.

Every night was different but the same, with a revolving cast of characters. Sometimes I would call Sasha and she would come and meet us at the pub for a few drinks, sometimes we would head out for a lavish dinner at a newly opened restaurant, running up a bill of several hundred dollars in the full confidence we would never see the check.

More often than not, dinner was a launching point for the rest of the night. At some point, someone – sometimes me – would say, "Want to get some blow?" I would hand over $50 to a guy who would materialise out of the night, and twenty minutes later be chopping out rails of coke in the bathroom. That was when you knew this was going to be a late one. That was also when I knew what our ultimate destination that night would be: Siberia.

It was through Chris that I met Tracey Westmoreland, the fearsome-looking bewhiskered ex-bouncer who owned Siberia, the notorious dive bar underneath the bridge where 40th Street crossed 9th Avenue.

Siberia was a crucial part of any New York night out with Chris. Sure, we would be made welcome at all the fancy bars and clubs around town – Marquee, Bungalow 8, Hiro – and even served a check-free bottle of vodka. But come 3am, all the glitz and the glamour could never rival the filthy lure of Siberia.

You walked along 40th Street until you saw the single red bulb marking the entrance. Pull open the door and step inside. Upstairs was the bar with the Harleys, downstairs there was a stage in a bare empty room with another bar propped crazily against the wall. The floor felt like liquidised chewing gum.

There were always little stories coming out of Siberia for *Page Six* – Jimmy Fallon and Horatio Sanz would sometimes get drunk there and Tracey always had great gossip about the machinations of the Hell's Kitchen nightlife world. The upshot was that I usually drank there for free.

The thing I really liked about Siberia, though, was that no one would bother me in there. No one in that place would criticise me or tell me I drank too much because there was always someone there drunker than me. I felt right at home in its dingy, graffiti-covered interior, which reminded me in a funny way of The Nostril, the old bomb shelter we used to smoke in back at Eton. It was almost impossible to get in trouble there. I only saw Tracey ever flip out twice. The first time was when I lit a pre-rolled joint I had in my pocket while I was sitting at the bar and he went ballistic. The second time was when he threw out some loud investment banker-types – all Brooks Brothers shirts and handmade shoes – for swearing. "No cursing!" he hollered as he pushed them out the door. "That's the rules of Siberia!" As he came back in he shook his head and sighed,

"Those fuckin' guys were really getting on my fuckin' nerves."

"Fuck 'em man," said Chris, and we all span back to our drinks.

If you got in a bad mood, or a good one, or you just wanted to let off some steam you could kick a hole in the wall or smash some bottles at Siberia and no one would raise an eyebrow. Siberia was the ultimate dive bar, a shabby, shitty, black hole – and it exerted an irresistible, magnetic pull on me.

-145 DAYS

I WOKE UP where I usually did these days, on the sofa, my sofa of shame. It was around 6am. I crept as quietly as I could into the bathroom to be sick, then brushed my teeth and got into bed with Sasha. It was Monday morning. Still, at least I didn't have to go into work. I tried not to think about the fact that I didn't really have any work.

"Did you have a fun night Monkey?" Sasha asked me.

"It was OK," I said. "Late, you know. I crashed out on the sofa. Sorry."

"Don't be sorry," she said.

Sasha always said stuff like this and I never knew what she meant. Was this OK? Or was it that this was definitely not OK and words weren't going to change that? I lay there in silence for a few minutes, the morning light filtering through the curtains, sheets of cotton nailed to the wall.

Neither of us were asleep. "Monk, I think I am going to have to stop drinking," I said.

"You don't have to stop," she said. "You just have to limit yourself. You just can't get totally wasted every night of the week."

"Yeah," I said, relieved I wouldn't have to quit after all.

And then I had a plan. "I know what, I'll just drink two or three drinks a night every night. And just get actually *drunk* one night a week." Pause. I rolled up on my arm and looked at Sasha and thought about the week ahead. There was a party tonight and the next night. I'd have to get drunk both nights. "Actually, *two* nights a week. I'll only get *drunk* two nights a week," I said. "Two nights a week is OK."

"Mmm," Sasha mumbled from her sleep. "Yes Monkey."

That plan worked well for the next two nights. I got drunk both nights.

It went wrong on the third night when I tried to just have two – or three – glasses of wine and ended up getting drunk again. Ah well, I thought, as I tried to catch the barman's eye, sitting at the bar in my local pub with Jean, the French manager of La Bonne Soupe restaurant across the street. I'd just have to quit. Someday, not now. It wasn't that bad yet. I could carry on for a couple more years.

"Another Jack Daniels please, Mark," I said.

"Tommy," said the Irish barman at my local. "First off me name's not Mark it's Michael and I've been tellin' you so all night. Secondly, no, I'm cutting you off, go home to your wife."

The rage exploded out of nowhere. "Fuck you man!" I shouted at the barman – Mark, Michael, whatever the fuck his name was. "Fucking tell me what to do you cunt!" I slammed my empty glass on the bar, but it wouldn't break.

He'd disappeared down the other end of the bar and just shouted back, "Mind how you go now."

Jean was on his feet and he was saying to me, "Hey, Tom, easy, easy."

"The amount of money I spend in this fucking place Jean, and that fucking cunt won't even give me a drink."

"Forget it, Tom," Jean was saying. "Forget it. Just go home."

It didn't look like I had any option, so I left. I walked up the block to my apartment and let myself in. Sasha was asleep. There was one beer in the fridge. I found an old bag of coke and racked up a couple of lines on the table.

I was fine. I just wanted one more drink. I'd go to the other bar on 54th Street and get one. As I opened the door to head out again I heard Sasha sleepily saying, "Monk?" from the bedroom. "Where are you going?"

"Won't be a minute," I said, walking out the door.

I stormed round to 54th Street. The bar was closed, shuttered, lights off. I considered my options. This part of town was dead at night. It was one thing I hated now that we had moved from the East Village to midtown. Nowhere to get a fucking drink. I could always go to Siberia.

And then the righteous anger welled up inside me. How the fuck could that asshole of a barman refuse to serve me? Wasn't I their best customer? Didn't I tip the bastard handsomely? I chewed my lip and ground my teeth furiously as I headed back to 55th Street. I walked up to the bar and tried the door. It was locked. I peered in the big glass window – and there they were, Jean and Michael-Mark-whatever-the-fuck his name was, laughing and chatting away. Fuckers.

I banged furiously on the window and they both jumped round in alarm. "Let me in!" I screamed, the rage surging round my system, feeling terrific. "Let me in! I just want a beer!"

Michael turned back to Jean and spoke to him. Jean shrugged. I walloped the window again. It trembled in its frame. "Oi, Michael, sorry I forgot your name. I just want a drink and then I'll go."

He came up to the window and shouted at me through the glass. "We're closed, Tommy boy. It's time for beddy-byes."

I struck the glass with the fleshy part of my fist again. Hard. "Let me in. Please."

"Don't go breakin' my windows now Tom for Christ's sake and makin' me get the police to fetch ya," Michael was saying.

"OK, fine," I said. "You won't let me in, I'll just stay here."

So I lay down on the ground outside the bar, parallel to the window. It was cold. I actually was in the gutter looking at the stars. He would have to let me in before I died, right?

I don't know how long I was there, seething with anger. But eventually Jean came out.

"Tom?" he asked, "Are you OK?"

I wouldn't answer. "Tom, it's me, Jean. The bar is closed. I'm going home. Do you want me to get Sasha?"

So the bar really was closed now. Suddenly I felt sober. What the hell was I doing? I stood up. "No man, sorry. I'm fine. Just fine," I said, and shuffled off home.

I got back inside and there were still three lines of coke on the table. Before I knew what I was doing, I rolled up a note and sniffed one down. I was fine. I didn't need this shit. I needed to go to bed. I swept the rest of the coke away with the edge of my hand. I rolled up a joint to calm me down.

Twenty minutes later I was searching for the white crumbs in the carpet, plucking them out on the end of my licked index finger with a surgeon's precision, thinking to myself, *None of this would have happened if Michael had just given me a goddamn drink.*

19

-130 DAYS

I T's THE MORNING after my birthday and the sun's coming up. I'm fifty stories above Madison Avenue, on the roof of my friend Brad's building and off my face. A head-height wall, about a foot thick, runs around the perimeter of the roof space. I am standing on it. Stunning view of the Empire State Building, I think to myself. I stretch my arms in the shape of a cross and I jump up in the air.

Some of my best friends in the world, including James, my old dealer, and Frank are visiting from the UK for my thirtieth birthday. It's been months in the planning and it turned out to be everything I wanted. A fabulous dinner, plenty of wine, and an eightball of cocaine to keep the drinking going.

James's face has gone white. He is shouting, "TOM GET DOWN GET THE FUCK DOWN MAN GET DOWN COME ON."

But I'm not going anywhere. I jump up and land on my perch again and grin at their panic. "Come on man, get up here! It's an awesome view."

I jump up in the air again and again. Up and down, up and down, on my foot-wide shelf, far above the city. I jump three inches. Six inches. Not quite a foot. A little gust of wind blows thrillingly. I rock back and forward, my arms outstretched and mock my friends, "Woooaahh!" I shout, pretending I'm overbalancing, teetering back and forth like a dancing Jesus on the cross.

Now Frank is shouting at me to get down too. James's tone is angry now.

"It's all right," I say to them, "I'm not going to jump off."

James puts his hand over his eyes, falls to one knee and says, "I can't fucking watch. Get the fuck down Tommy. This 'aint funny."

I laugh. It *is* funny. I look around the roof at the scene of utter debauchery. It must be five in the morning and we've brought a tiny fold-up table up here – it's about nine inches off the ground – to snort coke off. On the roof! There's a bottle of vodka and a bottle of gin. James, Frank, Brad and me are the last survivors of my thirtieth birthday party.

It really has been one of the legendary nights. About twenty-five of my friends came to Indochine, a restaurant in NoHo for dinner, then we toured the dive bars and clubs around the East Village, the big package of coke tucked snugly in the small pocket of my jeans next to my keys, which are tied to my belt loops by a green ribbon so I won't lose them. We headed back to Brad's as the sun came up, and now, here we are, on the roof, and I'm jumping in the air.

I share my birthday with my father. I've never observed Father's Day, but, because of this coincidence of birth dates, I still get one day a year when I am forced to contemplate my troubled relationship with my dad. I think this astrological quirk of having a mutual birthday is one of the main reasons I am still regularly in touch with my father. I am the only one of all his children who still speaks to him regularly. Once a year I feel like I have to call.

He never calls me. That's just not the way it works with my dad. If you wait for him to call you, you could be waiting a long time. I always call early. That way I can pretend that he would have called me later in the day. Of course he would.

About five years ago I called my dad on our birthday. I sang happy birthday down the phone.

"Oh, that's so sweet of you to call," he said, once I had finished. "Thanks so, so much."

I paused, waiting for him to say it. Nothing.

"Oh, that's OK," I said, eventually.

Say happy birthday to me you fucker. "How have you been?" I asked eventually.

"Oh, you know, pretty good."

Unbelievable. We were born on the *same day* for God's sakes. My mum has even told me about the party which I broke up by arriving halfway through.

And he can't even wish me a happy birthday. I hate him for this. But I resent him even more for the fact that he never, ever calls me, I always have to call him. I hate him for the fact that he never, not once, ever asks me how I am doing, or asks what I am up to in my life. He never asks "How's Fred?" or "How's Josh?"

Instead, I say, "Fred's doing well. He's at Oxford you know." I say, "I got a new job," and I say, "I had a piece in the paper today, I'll send you a copy," but I never do.

When I was fourteen and my parents had separated I desperately wanted to speak to my dad. I had his address in the South of France and I sent him a letter from Eton, asking him to call me ten days later on the school phone box at 7pm. I gave the phone number for the phone box and, ten days later, I got there at 6.45.

I was sure he would call. I held the handset in my left hand, talking animatedly, with my right hand over the catch, so that no one would throw me out of the phone booth before my dad rang.

I had the best conversation of my life with my dad that night. Yes, I was fine thanks. Upset about you leaving like that, though, of course. Why did you do it? Oh, right, right, I understand. But how could you leave me and Fred and Josh? What about our school fees and everything else? Oh, OK. When will I see you again? Oh really? Oh, great, great, I can't wait.

It was just a shame he wasn't on the other end of the line. At 7.30 I gave up. I lifted my hand off the catch and hung the handset up. I walked back across the road to my schoolhouse biting my lip.

I told my mum what had happened and she told Dr Harrison. He cornered me one night, saying, "Now Sykes, I hear you're upset because your father failed to ring you at a telephone box?" He looked at me like I was an idiot.

The tears started welling up and I gritted my teeth together. I felt hot, like I was guilty or stupid or had done something wrong. I wanted to deny it. And the way Harrison was talking to me was so patronising.

"Come into my office," he said, grinning at me from behind his half-moon glasses.

I stood in front of his massive wooden desk. His chair squeaked as he leant back in it, his hands behind his head, sweat patches around his underarms. "Well, Thomas, the two things nobody can be responsible for in life are his name or his parents," Harrison grinned at me brightly, delighted with his witticism. I remember his breath smelled of alcohol that night. A tear started rolling down my nose. I swallowed hard.

"There's no need to blub about it, Sykes. It's not your fault."

I turned and walked out of his office, blinded by the reservoir of tears I was trying to keep in my eyes. I couldn't decide who I hated more, my father or Dr Harrison.

I wrote an angry letter to my father, scrawling out in my fifteen-year-old hand, "Why the fuck did you do it?" and, "You know what I think? I think you decided you just couldn't be fucked."

My dad didn't answer. When I finally confronted him about the letter, he said that I had become "abusive" and so he wouldn't respond.

This I couldn't believe. Now, it seemed, I could talk to my father only in language appropriate for a customer service manager, or I risked getting the line disconnected.

I couldn't face being shut off entirely, so I played along instead. Whenever I would meet my dad I would never suggest I was unhappy. I only asked him once or twice why he had abandoned me and my family. He exploded in rage and almost walked out of the restaurant we were in each time. I learnt to leave it alone. We talked instead about other things. My dad joking and laughing and telling me funny stories about his friends and acquaintances. His car. His new house. His company. It was always his life, I noticed, not mine. He still never asked me a thing.

So my birthday has always been a mixed-up day for me, making a phone call instead of waiting for one that may never come. Best dealt with by getting obliterated and doing something stupid, like jumping as high as I could in the air several hundred feet above the cold, hard tarmacadam.

Jump. If I fell, he probably wouldn't find out for a week or two anyway.

Jump. I might be like him.

Jump. And every year, on this day of all days, *my birthday*, I have to spend all day thinking about him.

When I was fourteen I started crying. I cried the whole time. Someone would only have to mention my dad – or *their* dad – and I would feel hot, feel the welling begin. I was embarrassed to be such a baby. To *blub*. It was shameful.

So I stopped crying. I didn't cry for a long, long time.

Eventually I climb down off the wall. James is pleased. He throws his arms around me. But all I can think is that I want to speak to my dad. There's a conversation I need to have with him. I need to just sit down, and ask him one very simple question: Why didn't you ever care to see your kids, Dad?

I got home that night at about 7am. Frank and James stayed out on the roof, drinking until after the sun came up and then fell asleep up there.

It was June, in New York, and when they came up to my apartment the next night they were both so sunburnt they looked like they had been involved in an industrial beetroot juice spillage. Frank showed me where his T-shirt had ridden up his chest while he slept, giving him a ring of livid sunburn on his stomach which ended just below his solar plexus like a punchline.

"It was totally bizarre when we woke up," said James. "There were two really neat and trim gay guys up there, looking at us in disgust. And there were just bottles of warm gin everywhere."

James is punctuating the story with his throaty, London chuckle, "I'd cut my foot and there was blood everywhere. And Frank and me were just lying in the middle of it all, totally passed out. I woke up and I saw these guys, and sort of nudged Frank, 'Frank! Frank!'…"

Frank took up the story, trying to control his laughter, "And I was like, 'What?' and I tried to stand up, and my sunburn was just like, Aaarghh!"

We all laughed. Then I said to James, "I can't believe I was jumping up and down on that wall, man."

And James's face crumpled. First it went white. Then he scowled; an expression somewhere between fury, sorrow and pity. He just said, "Fucking hell, Tommy. That wasn't funny."

I'd booked us into dinner at Jean-Luc's on the Upper West Side. He gave us the private room. It took about six bottles of wine just to take the edge off that night.

20

-100 DAYS

CHRIS AND I had been invited on a three-day, all-expenses-paid press trip to Amsterdam by Heineken.

"Oh my God," said Paula, when she found out where we were going for the weekend. "You two are going to Amsterdam? With a beer company? Are they out of their minds?"

Well, yes, they were, but they needed coverage.

I had been to Amsterdam a few times as a teenager on weed-smoking holidays. It was easy to get there from London, and although the grass wasn't much cheaper, the fact that you could just buy it in coffee shops and openly skin up right there on the pavement was sufficiently novel to keep us coming back. As my flight droned over the Atlantic, I tried to sleep, but memories of the city had me too excited to get much rest. I felt the way I often did before a big party – excited, but nervous about the potential extent of the mayhem that lay in store.

The first night we arrived, a Thursday, I dragged Chris out to go and shoot some pool. His bag had got lost on the flight, so all he had was the clothes he was standing up in and a credit card. Not his credit card, though – he used Ron, the PR guy's credit card. We hit a coffee shop first and got some cannabis. Underneath a glass counter top, there were thirty different types of hash and herbal marijuana. I bought a few grams of charis – a particularly potent Indian hashish resin – from the hippy behind the counter, and sat down at a table to skin up with a cup of herbal tea. All the coffee shops in Amsterdam have lame names, many of them harking back to 1970s psychedelia. We were sitting in the Doors café, just across the street from the Pink Floyd. If I opened a coffee shop here I'd call it the Funkadelic and play Maggot Brain all day.

The Doors was decorated like a student stoner's flat – drapes on the walls, drapes over the chairs, and maybe a total of about 60 watts of light illuminating the whole place. In fact, skinning up in there reminded me of being in The Nostril all those years ago.

I skinned up a joint – expertly splitting a cigarette and emptying the tobacco into the rolling papers, burning the sweet-smelling hash and crumbling it on top. It smelt vegetal. It was sticky, oily, and I had to rub my fingers to get it all off. I felt the anticipation of the first hit building in my mind. I stuck down the paper and smoothed out the joint.

I lay back on the banquette and stuck the joint between my lips. I sparked the lighter, touched the end of the joint to the flame and inhaled. The joint crackled like a forest fire.

The first puff of a joint is always the best. I visualised the thick, herbal smoke spiralling down my bronchial tubes, into my lungs, filling them all with the beautiful, deadly, narcotic toxins.

One second, two seconds … and there it was. The drug hit my brain and I was back in the zone. I exhaled a plume of purple smoke. I took another few hits and passed it on to Chris.

The Doors café only played The Doors, which must have been tiresome if you worked there but made it a fun place to visit. I lay back, my head not spinning so much as revolving slightly, and wondered, as I often did, what it was that marijuana really did to me. I had smoked dope since I was fourteen, a regular smoker by the age of sixteen. At seventeen and eighteen I was buying an ounce and selling seven-eighths of it on, getting a free eighth for myself. I weighed it out on an old set of postal scales I had found in the attic at home.

I quit smoking dope three times in my life. The first was when I had to do my A-levels at eighteen (three months). The second was when I had to do my final exams in Edinburgh when I was twenty-two (three months again). The third had been when I came to New York, aged twenty-nine (two weeks). I had meant to stop for good in New York, but once I found out where to buy grass, the amount crept back up until I was smoking half an ounce a week once again. There had been another enforced interval when I had to get a new dealer because my old one had discovered that I worked for the *Post*.

"Huh, Tom Sykes of the *New York Post*?" he said one day when he came into my apartment and I had left a copy of that day's paper out, "Interesting. Very interesting."

My new dealer worked for another paper across town. An ounce cost me about $100. By now it only lasted just over a week.

Chris passed the joint back to me. I lay down on the banquette, stretched out full length and brought the joint down to my lips. I shut one eye against the smoke, and squinted through the other as the tip glowed bright red. A burning lump of hash fell on my face. I hardly felt it, but brushed it away automatically. This was some good shit, I thought to myself, laughing at how clichéd I sounded. But then again, I was in the Doors Café in Amsterdam, and Jim Morrison was saying, "Out here, in the desert, we are stoned immaculate." I could use a little cliché. I cracked open an eye and looked at Chris. "Man," I said, parodying my thoughts, "This is some goo-o-o-d sh-i-i-et."

We finished the joint and I started rolling another one.

"You want another one?" Chris asked, incredulously. His eyes looked like fried eggs, and I guessed mine were the same.

Yes, I wanted another one. And another after that. I wanted to sit here all day and get wrecked. Wasn't that what everyone wanted to do? Wasn't that the whole point of being in Amsterdam?

I opened my mouth to speak but nothing came out. So I just looked at Chris and said, "Uuuh??"

I carried on rolling up. When it was done I fired it up and passed it to Chris. "No, man, I'm stoned. I won't be able to see. That's enough."

Enough? Enough? What did *that* mean?

I smoked the rest of the joint myself. I sat up on the banquette but my limbs felt too big for it. Chris had started talking to some people on the table next to us. I wanted to join in but I couldn't think of anything to say. I moved my mouth but my voice wouldn't work. I wished I wasn't so stoned. But seeing as I was, I figured another joint might make me feel better. I started sticking together the papers frantically.

"Oh my god you're having another one?" asked Chris. I nodded dumbly. "We've got a lot of weed to smoke over the next few days," I said, waving the bag in front of me, my voice thin and cracked.

Chris stood up. "All right man. Whatever. I'm going to check out the city a bit." He walked out the door.

I looked around the coffee shop. Everyone else was in twos or threes, I was the only person on my own. I carried on rolling up the joint. I smoked it. I sat there, stoned. My heart was racing. Everyone seemed to be looking at me out of the corner of their eye. I wished I had a newspaper to read. Something to occupy me. An excuse to stay here.

But this was how getting stoned went these days. Stage One, skinning up the first joint: excitement. Stage Two, smoking the first few puffs: sweet release. Stage Three, actually being stoned for the rest of the day: racing heart, paranoia, feeling incapable of doing anything, crushing depression, smoking more, on my own, to try and feel better and just feeling worse. That's where I was now. I didn't know what to do with myself, but I managed to make it back to the hotel across the road. I crashed out in my room, justifying it to myself by saying that I was suffering jet lag.

When I woke up a little over three hours later as it was getting dark, I felt a lot better. I knew from experience that it took me three hours without a joint to stop feeling actively stoned, although most mornings I still had a cloudy head. Smoked-over, I called it.

I reached out for the phone and called Chris's room.

"Yo," I said when he picked up. "Wanna go hit some bars?"

I was determined to leave the weed behind. But I couldn't resist having one quick hit before I left the room. I met Chris in the lobby five minutes later. Chris was dressed head to toe in H&M where he had bought an entire holiday wardrobe to replace his lost case. Cargo pants, primary colour T-shirt, the works.

"You look like Avril Lavigne," I said.

"I feel ridonculous," Chris conceded. "But my suitcase still hasn't arrived. I didn't want to spend too much dough."

"Come on Skater Boy. Let's shoot some pool." I said.

The pool table was located in the basement of the bar we wound up in, accessed by a particularly steep, narrow and winding staircase. In the middle of the third frame

Chris went upstairs to get some beers and came back down with a huge crash as he fell down the stairs.

He limped around a bit that evening, but the next day he pulled up his T-shirt and showed me the bruise. It was the nastiest thing I had ever seen. It started halfway up his left buttock and was the size and shape of a rugby ball, spreading up to his kidney. It went from blue, to black to green to a deathly yellow. Chris limped around the whole weekend moaning, "I got a broken ass."

On the Friday night we went to a coffee shop where I got so stoned that during dinner I became convinced that a DJ called Speedy, who was also on the press trip for a regional radio station, was trying to kill me. "Speedy wants me dead," I kept saying to anyone who would listen over dinner. "I don't know what I've done but he wants me dead!"

The big party was on the Saturday – Heineken were sponsoring an event with the dire name Amsterjam. On the bus on the way there a fat, sweat-pant wearing American woman in her forties stood up in the bus and started officiously saying, "Testing-testing-one-two-three," into her microphone.

"OK, hi!" she said, holding heavily on to the coat racks as we swung through Amsterdam's twisting streets. "So we are going to Amsterjam and we here at Heineken, we would really appreciate it if in your stories and broadcasts you could try and mention the Heineken slogan at least twice. Remember, the slogan is, 'It's All About the Beer'. We also

WHAT DID I DO LAST NIGHT?

would appreciate it you didn't talk too much about the coffee shops and the marijuana situation."

"Can we mention magic mushrooms?" I asked, shoving a handful into my mouth and pulling a face while I chewed them down.

The festival was actually pretty good. I was buzzing nicely off the mushrooms. I had stacks of weed to smoke, and I found a UK drum and bass tent where I sat for hours. I shared a joint with some Dutch guys and lay on my back in the sun, feeling my arms stretched out and the sun beating down on me.

Towards 7pm, with the sun going down, I ran into the fat lady whose main job seemed to be to corral us. When she saw me she pounced. "Where have you been?" she yelled, grabbing my arm. 'C'mon, it's time to go. The bus is leaving now."

"Whoa, whoa, take your hands off me please," I asked. Everything was happening in slow motion and I felt very calm. "I'm not coming back on the bus," I said.

"Oh yes you are," she said, sweat rolling off her face. "You *have* to."

Whenever anyone tells me I have to do something I do the opposite. A taxi driver told me I had to use the curbside door once, so I used the one on the roadside instead. I escaped death by fractions of an inch as a blaring eighteen-wheeler jinked past me.

I looked at the fat woman telling me to get on the bus. "Listen," I said. "You're in the wrong cultural mindset. I'm a European. I love festivals. I get festivals. It's just getting dark and this one is just about to start. You are crazy to go now. The rubbish bit is just finishing. This is where it gets good. If you want to go, go. I'm staying." I paused.

It's really, really hard to talk sense when you are tripping on magic mushrooms. You can do it for a bit, then you just lose it. So when she asked me, "How will you get home?" Instead of saying, "I'll take the train, like everyone else," I replied, "I met some Dutch friends of mine. They said they'll give me a lift."

By this time we had been joined by the New York PR, Ron, who asked me, "Well, where are they?"

I looked around me and looked back at Ron. He was zooming in and out of focus. "Actually, they don't exist. I just made them up." I sighed, "Really though, I'll be fine. I'll take the train."

Ron tried to argue with me. He was halfway through making his next point when I said, "Look, sorry. Have to go." I ran ducking and weaving into the crowd.

The festival was awesome. I gobbled up mushrooms and beer and went back to the drum and bass tent for the rest of the night.

"Oh ... my ... oh my golly gosh," the London MC yelled down the mic. I roared my approval, and felt home-sick. What was I doing here? What was I doing in New York? Just going out to dinner the whole time?

About midnight the festival closed down so I just followed the crowd to the exits. The Dutch, I thought to myself as I climbed on a train, are so incredibly organised that really, there had been no need for anyone to worry about me. They'd be a bit pissed off, but what the hell? They were the ones who had brought us to Amsterdam, the land of legal drugs.

I got back to the hotel. I was still tripping pretty hard when I walked into the lobby at about 2am. It was quiet. The concierge behind the desk hardly raised his eyes at me. I was starting to feel a little bad now. I hoped the PR people were not too worried about me. I should call up to their room and say sorry.

I tried to explain to the desk clerk what I wanted but he wouldn't put a call through for me. Seeing as how I was resting my chin flat on his desk, I can't, in retrospect, really blame him.

But then I saw a board in the lobby with the Amsterjam logo on it and a twenty-four-hour number. I'd call that, let them know I was OK.

The number rang a few times, then it clicked, switched to an American dial phone and a woman four thousand miles away in California where it was 5pm on Saturday afternoon picked up the phone. "Hello?" she said frantically, "What is it? What's the matter? Why are you calling the emergency line?"

"Everything's fine," I said. It was dawning on me that maybe this call wasn't such a smart move.

"Who is it?" said the lady at the other end of the phone sounding close to tears. "What's happened. Tell me what's happened. My god, I knew Amsterdam was a bad idea!"

"No really, everything is fine." I said. Oh shit. This was bad. The woman on the other end of the line was freaking out big time. "I was just calling to say I managed to get a bus home to the hotel."

"Who are you?" screamed the woman. "Why the hell are you calling? Just tell me."

"OK, look," I said, "My name is Tom Sykes. I work for the *Post*. And I stayed behind at the rave and now I am back at the hotel. I was just calling because it seemed like everyone was really worried about me."

The phone went silent at the other end. "Hello?" I asked eventually.

"Let me get this straight," said the woman, who had now metamorphosed from a sobbing, emotional wreck into an icy block of corporate communications, "You're calling the emergency line to report the fact that *there's no emergency?*"

"Well, yeah, I suppose so," I said, "But, there *could* have been an emergency, right? If you think about it."

"OK Mr Sykes," she said, after another long pause, "I am so glad you're OK. Why don't you run along to bed now."

-99 DAYS

i WOKE UP in the morning feeling unbearably toxic, dislocated and spaced out from the combination of mushrooms, beer and weed.

I'd been awake about two minutes when I remembered the late-night phone call. Why did every single night out always have to end in such embarrassment and disaster? Why couldn't I drink like a gentleman? I stood vacantly in the shower, water beating down on my back and head for an age as I pondered my stupidity. Well, with any luck, no one on the trip would have found out about it. Maybe the woman I had spoken to had just forgotten about it. Why had I given the woman my name? I bumped my head gently against the tiles and cursed my idiocy.

Eventually I went down for breakfast.

I had just sat down at a table with a glass of orange juice when a guy named Mac, who was another one of the Heineken coordinators, came and pulled out a chair and sat down at my table.

I stared down at my fruit salad. I wouldn't look up. After thirty seconds or so, Mac asked the top of my head, "Tom, did you call the emergency number last night to report that you got a train back to Amsterdam and were home safe?"

Very, very slowly I raised my head. I met Mac's eyes. They were clear and bright. I knew my own were hopelessly bloodshot, verging on yellow. I was a mess.

"Erm, yeah, I did. Sorry man." I scratched my head apologetically and pulled a pained face.

"Tom," Mac said fixing me right in the eye with a steely gaze. "I think you are actually OK as a person and I quite like you. But you are the most ridiculous man I have ever met."

I cracked a smile. He was kidding right? He wasn't really mad at me, surely?

But Mac wasn't smiling. Not one bit. I tried to break the atmosphere by asking, "Ridiculous as in funny or in the original sense of the word, as in one who inspires ridicule?"

"The original sense of the word," Mac replied. "The bus to the airport leaves in thirty minutes exactly. That is, unless you would rather make your own way there?"

21

-96 DAYS

THE THING that amazed me most about *Page Six* was how little you had to write about someone's event for them to be ecstatically happy. Chris's write-up of our Amsterdam sortie was a classic of the genre. "We hear that Amsterdam was the place for dance-music fans to be at the weekend," he wrote, before going on to describe the festival in about four lines, making sure to mention the sponsor's name. I was pleased to note he hadn't written, "It's all about the beer."

I studied the entry in amazement. "Is that it?" I asked Chris.

"That's it man," he said.

Page Six had power. One night I was drinking on 9th Avenue with Sasha at a place called the Brite Bar, which was right next to Marquee, when the owner, a guy named John Libonati, heard I worked for *Page Six*. He stopped over at our table and said he'd pick up the tab for our drinks.

"Thanks mate," I said.

John signalled to the bar to indicate that we wouldn't be requiring a bill. It was a gesture I had become used to seeing since arriving in New York. John combined the international "Bill please" squiggle with a finger pointed at himself and half-second eyebrow lift.

"So, you're on *Page Six*, right?"

"Yeah," I say. "I just do one day a week there. Got any stories for us?"

"Well," he says, "Bjork was in here the other day. She was really nice, had a bit of a party. She's kind of crazy, you know."

I nod. "Wearing a dead swan to the Oscars was kind of a red flag," I say.

"Well, the next day her assistant calls up and says she has left her coat – it's a fur coat – behind. Can she come round and get it? So I go look in the cupboard, and sure enough, there it is. So I get back on the phone and say, sure, she can come round any time."

I leant back in my seat and took a sip of my drink. "So what, Bjork forgets her coat?"

"Yeah, right, but the thing is, a few days after the assistant has been round to get the coat we get another message from the assistant saying can we please return Bjork's iPod. I call up and say there was no iPod. And then they basically accuse me of having stolen her iPod. I tell them we don't have Bjork's iPod. Then I hear Bjork, in the background, going on and on and on about how we have stolen her iPod and want to steal all her music or something. In the end, I just hang up. Five days later we get a very sheepish message. It's Bjork's assistant. 'Uh, sorry,' she says, 'Bjork found the iPod. It slipped down behind the seat in the car. Sorry about that.' I can't believe she thought my staff would steal her belongings out of her coat jacket! What, did she think we were going to put it on eBay or something?"

By this time everyone at the table is laughing. And I say, "Yeah, that's a funny item. I'll see what I can do."

The next day was a Friday, so I wrote the item up and it ran on Monday.

On Tuesday, the phone rang. It was John. "Hey, Tom," he said, "I just wanted to say thank you so much for the great item on *Page Six*. The bar's been packed ever since. And you wouldn't believe the calls I've been getting."

"What calls?" I asked.

"Calls about the story from all over the world. Newspapers from London to Brazil. And in Iceland they have gone crazy! Crazy! We've even done telephone interviews with Icelandic TV stations. It's incredible."

It turned out that all the other newspaper gossip columnists in the world read *Page Six* online every day to get ideas and stories. They'd liked the Bjork item and ran it themselves. Then the really industrious ones had looked up the number of John's bar and called for more details. I checked the internet while John was on the phone and there were over 500 different accounts of my story. "We just stopped answering the phone after a while," he said. "Thanks so much. Come here any time. We'll take care of you."

"I might just take you up on that John," I said.

-89 DAYS

WHEN SOMEONE offers you a free drink because you've done something useful for them, it's best to take them up on the offer sooner rather than later, while their gratitude is still ripe. So a week later, when I was out with Sasha and our friends Emma and Jules, I asked, "Anyone want to get drunk for free?" and we hopped in a cab to the Brite bar. The place was heaving when we walked in, but John swiftly cleared us a table and got a waiter over to take our orders.

I was in the mood to get drunk, and drinking fast, even by my standards. I knocked back about five or six cocktails in the two hours or so we were there. It was Fleet Week in New York, when the Navy docks in the town for a week, and a couple of twenty-one-year-old sailors were standing by the bar looking nervous and out of place, glowing white in their full uniform. I walked up to them and asked if I could get them a drink, as a mark of respect for the fine, unselfish service they were rendering the country. They accepted, of course, and we got chatting.

More than anything, it turned out, they wanted to go to Marquee. They had read on *Page Six* that Marquee was a hangout for everyone from Paris Hilton to Ja Rule, and they had come over to 9th Avenue from their ship, or wherever they were staying, only to be turned away at the door.

I saw an opportunity to be magnaninmous. "I'll take you in lads," I said. "You wanna go now?"

Sure, they said, skulling their drinks and grabbing their coats. "Then let's go," I said.

"I'm just going to get these boys into Marquee," I explained to Sasha and our friends. "Won't be a minute."

She looked up at me in confusion, but I was already out of the door.

There was a mob of maybe 200 people trying to get past Rich, the doorman at Marquee. The girls were dressed in tiny strips of chiffon, the guys were either merchant bankers in suits or hipsters wearing vintage AC/DC T-shirts. My two sailors were wearing full uniform – white sailor suits set off by those bizarre round hats.

No matter, I was Tom Sykes from the *New York Post*. I fought my way to the front of the mob and caught Rich, the bouncer's eye. He came over.

"Hey Tom, how many are you?"

"Just three," I said, pointing at the two sailors.

Rich paused for one-twentieth of a second, looked at my seafaring buddies – who really looked very uncool – took a deep breath and said, "OK, come on in."

The sailors could hardly contain themselves, and suddenly I saw my world from their perspective. The hundreds of pairs of eyes enviously staring at them as they walked the red carpet into the club. The doorman, who just hours earlier had ignored them as worthless specimens, was now shaking their hands and introducing himself. The people inside the club, waiting to pay their cover charge to get in, wondered who we were as the owner, a guy called Noah Tepperberg, came out to greet us and led us directly into the booming interior, stuffed to the gills with the beautiful people of Manhattan. Once I had got them inside, I bade the sailors farewell and zipped back out the door to the Brite bar. I got back to my table flushed with success and selflessness.

"What was all that about?" Jules asked me.

"They couldn't get into Marquee so I took them in," I said. "Military men deserve a break."

We had a few more drinks. We were all slaughtered. Everyone stood up and got ready to leave.

"Fancy going to Marquee?" I asked Sasha when we got onto the street. "I want to check up on my sailors."

"No, I'm tired Monkey," she said. "I want to go home."

I pulled a face.

"You go on if you want," she said.

I pulled out my phone and rang Chris.

"Where are you man?"

"We're at Marquee," he said, the music booming in the background. "Come on over."

"I'll be there in five," I said, snapping the phone shut. I turned to tell Sasha the plan, but she was already walking away to a cab. Sod it, I thought, I'm going out.

-88 DAYS

THE NEXT THING I remember I was in my building, standing outside the door to my apartment. I always carried my keys tied to my belt loops with a bit of green ribbon so I wouldn't lose them. The ribbon had the Paul Smith logo on it. It had come off a box containing a beautiful pink shirt my sisters Lucy and Alice had given me for my birthday.

I was confused. The door wouldn't open. The key went into the keyhole all right, but it just wouldn't turn. I checked the keys. I had the right one. I tried it again. The lock wouldn't budge. Swaying back and forth outside the door, I tried to figure out what was going on. I knew that when the door was open, there was a catch on the side which you could flip down to deadlock the mechanism. Sasha must have activated it. It wasn't the kind of thing you could do by accident. She must have locked me out to punish me for not coming home on time.

I rapped on the door, hard, with my knuckles. "Monkey!" I shouted. "Sorry I am so late, please can you let me in."

No answer. No movement inside the apartment. I knocked again, harder. "Monkey, let me in!"

Nothing. I walloped the door, hard, and shouted again. "Sasha! Come on! This isn't funny. I know you're in there."

Bitch! I kicked the door. It bounced in its frame. "Sasha! Please let me in." Silence.

I waited a few seconds and then I booted the door as hard as I fucking could and yelled for Sasha at the top of my voice. When she still didn't answer, I decided that if she wasn't going to let me in then I was going to kick the door down. I leaned my bum against the banister and kicked, *Whack! Whack! Whack!*

The whole door was shaking now, and a bit of plaster showered down on the carpet. "Monkey!" I screamed at the top of my lungs. "Let me in or I swear I'll break down the door!"

Nothing.

I gave the door my biggest, most powerful kick, screamed one more time, and then I gave up. It could be worse, I figured. At least I was inside, under cover. She'd have to let me in when she went out in the morning. Christ, though, I suddenly realised, tomorrow's Friday. *Bitch!* I had to work. I checked my watch. 5am. I'd better get some sleep. At least it was warm. I lay down on the carpet and dozed off.

I was dreaming that someone was kicking my feet. Then I realised that someone was kicking my feet. I opened my eyes, saw three guns being pointed at me, and the shouting started.

"Police! Don't *fucking* move man!"

I started to sit up.

"Lie down! Don't fucking move, put your hands behind your head, now, now, do it, DO IT!"

The black holes where the gun barrels ended were all I could see. I stretched my hands up so they were level with my head on the carpet. "What's going on?" I asked. I was so drunk I swore I was about to laugh. This was absurd. Had Sasha called the *cops* on me?

I don't know how long I lay there before the cops put their guns back in their holsters. There were three of them, and they all seemed short, stocky and powerfully built.

One of them stepped up over me, his feet either side of my thorax. "What's your name?" he was asking. "What's your name, what are you doing here?"

"Hi, I'm Tom," I began. "And I live here. I am trying to get into my apartment but my wife has locked me out because I am too drunk. I think. Or else the lock is broken."

"You live here?" the cop said, relaxing visibly. "Where are the keys?"

I started to reach down to my jeans pocket where I kept the keys attached to me, and the shouting started again. The cop standing over me had whipped out his gun and I actually heard him cock it, *cher-chik*, as all three of them yelled, *"Don't fucking move."*

The gun was about ten centimetres from my face. I could smell metal and cordite, but still it didn't seem real. I was so drunk and it was just too weird.

"Sorry, man," I said, lifting my hands up again. I raised them up and down a few times, like I was lifting a particularly light set of weights, and smiled hopefully at the cop. He didn't smile back. I stopped doing the weight-lifting mime.

"The keys are tied to my jeans," I said, pointing with my eyes.

Very, very slowly, the cop put his gun away a second time. He reached down in the same slow motion and grabbed the keys. Then he unsheathed a huge hunting knife, and sliced the green ribbon which tied my keys to my belt loop with one smooth movement. He tried the door. Nothing.

"See?" I said. "She's done something to the door."

The cop looked down at me, pinned against the shit-brown carpet, stepped over me and walked up the stairs with the keys. One of the other two cops still had his gun trained on me. I heard a *clunk* as a bolt slipped back upstairs. Then I heard him walk heavily down the stairs. He dropped the keys on my chest as he stepped over me. He stopped when he reached my feet.

"You're on the wrong floor," he said. "You live one flight up." I looked at him aghast. Then he pointed at the door I had been kicking the living daylights out of earlier.

"Your neighbours, who live *here*, called us because they thought someone was trying to kill them. It's lucky you passed out or you may well not be alive."

With that, he turned and all three cops walked down the stairs. The last one turned, looked at me, and said, "You fucking idiot." He said it without pity, without resentment, without humour. Just a simple statement of fact.

I picked myself up and walked up the last flight of stairs. I wandered into the apartment and woke up Sasha.

"Didn't you hear me?" I said. "I had three cops pointing at me. *Three cops were pointing at me!* I could have been killed."

"I can't understand what you are saying, Tommy," Sasha said. "Three cops what? Pointing at you?"

I gave up and walked into the sitting room, lay down on the sofa of shame and fell asleep.

I woke up the next day at 8am and went through to the bedroom and curled up against Sasha. At 10am, my alarm went off – I had no memory of setting it – and I sat up in bed. Shit. It was Friday. I had to get to work.

Sasha stirred next to me. "Tommy, what happened last night? I couldn't get any sense out of you. You were just going on and on about some cops pointing at you."

"Pointing *guns* at me," I laughed. I didn't have a hangover. I felt high. Must be all the adrenaline still coursing through my body.

"*What?*" Sasha said. "Guns?"

"Yeah," I said, laughing. "I couldn't get into the apartment and so I was trying to kick down the door. I thought you had locked me out because I was so late coming back. So I went to sleep in the passageway, and the next thing I knew there were three cops standing over me cocking their guns."

Sasha looked at me sleepily. I was grinning from ear to ear. She said, "Jesus, Tom," and rolled over to go back to sleep.

All right for some, I thought. I had to get to work to pay for this high-rolling lifestyle. I jumped out of bed and into the shower and threw some clothes on. I tied my keys back on to my jeans and walked to the *Post*. I didn't have any kind of hangover, although I felt lightheaded. I kept replaying the previous night's events in my head over and over again. The funniest bit was the way that the cop had just looked over his shoulder on the way out and said, "You fucking idiot." He'd said it so flat, with no drama or irritation in his voice, just pure condescension. The way he just tossed it out there made me think I was probably the third or fourth stairwell-sleeper of the night.

It was hot walking down 6th Avenue. It was going to be a sweaty day in New York. It was a relief to push through the revolving door into the air-conditioned cool of the lobby.

I took the elevator up to the tenth floor and walked down to my desk in the far corner of the office. I sat down at my chair and began firing up the computer and checking my messages, looking for items I could put on the list for the editorial meeting that Richard had to attend in half an hour. I was impatient to boast about my story, but I knew from experience there was no point trying to discuss anything in the frantic half-hour before conference.

About midday, as the pages for the weekend were starting to fall into place, the banter started.

"You were drunk last night man," said Chris. "You were crazy in Marquee."

"What was I doing?" I asked.

"Well, I think you were pretending to do a shit in the flowerpots at one stage. That's when I moved away. It was pretty funny though."

"Yeah, and you were wasted at Bungalow," said Paula.

I'd been to Bungalow? First I knew about that.

"You won't believe what happened to me when I got home," I said.

"What?" they both asked.

"Well, I couldn't get into my apartment and I passed out on the stairwell. Next thing I know there are three cops kicking me awake and shaking guns in my face."

"What?" said Chris, laughing. "You ended up at gunpoint last night?"

"Yeah man," I said, and told him as much of my story as I could remember. I finished, "And then, this cop, he's walking down the stairs, and he just looks at me and says, 'You fucking idiot.' Just like that. It was a heavy-duty night."

Chris was laughing. "That's ridonculous," he snorted, and we all turned back to our work.

Half an hour later I asked Paula if she wanted to go for a smoke. Once the doors shut in the elevator, she turned to me and said, "Tom, be careful with that story."

"What?" I said. "Why?"

"Think about it, Tom," she said, sounding exasperated. "If someone at the *Times* or the *Daily News* did that and we found out about it, we'd run it. Embarrass them. Maybe lose them their job."

Her words hung between us in the elevator silence until we pinged open on the ground floor. We stepped out.

"I guess you're right. It wouldn't be that funny then, would it?"

And Paula kind of exploded. "Fuck no. What – you think it's funny having cops nearly shooting you? Are you fucking *crazy*? And you are going around *telling everyone* about it like it's some kind of funny story? Are you out of your *mind*?"

I puffed on my cigarette, trying to finish it as quickly as possible and get back inside.

The hangover hit me about 3.30 that afternoon. I started deteriorating fast. I didn't get a headache but I began to feel seriously sick in the stomach. I started to see what Paula meant. Being threatened at gunpoint wasn't funny at all, actually. How could my judgement have been so off? The air was fetid and heavy. I went out to the diner down the block to get a grilled cheese sandwich and a coffee about 4pm, but the weariness got worse.

The problem with working Fridays on *Page Six* was that we had to do three columns – for Saturday, Sunday and Monday, and rarely finished before 7.30pm. Once we had written the items, we had to wait while Richard edited and laid out the pages in case there were any questions about our stories (which there usually were).

The good thing about Fridays was that Braden Keil, the restaurant writer, would usually open a bottle of wine at about 6pm.

On this particular Friday, I was desperate for some alcohol to fight off the hangover, so when Braden wandered down to our end of the office with a bottle, some plastic cups and a big grin, I sighed with relief. A few sips of wine was all it took for me to start to feel better. After three or four half-full plastic cups I was fine.

"Hey Chris," I said, "You want to go to Langan's for a pint after work?"

"I dunno man," he said, "I might go home and get some food first." Then he stopped, looked at me and said, "Hang on – you want to go *out*?"

"Yeah," I said, "Just a couple to take the edge off it, you know."

I got to Langan's and stepped up to the bar to order. I didn't have any money in my checking account, so I pushed my British Visa card across the bar. I felt guilty. The house-fund money was almost empty now, it had just a few hundred pounds left in it, but sod it, I needed a drink. After a few pints I started to feel a bit hyper. I had hardly eaten but the thought of food made me feel sick and I wasn't hungry. My phone rang and I looked at the display. It was Sasha.

"I'd better take this," I said to Chris, and stepped outside. I told Sasha I'd be home in half an hour.

At 5am I was racing back from Siberia up 6th Avenue, trying to beat the sunrise, preparing for another night of broken sleep on my sofa of shame.

22

-54 DAYS

My SISTER ALICE was eight months pregnant, and she and her boyfriend Chris Floyd – Floydy – decided to have one last weekend away before life, as they had known it in all its carefree, childless glory, came to an end. They rented a car and took off for a boutique hotel in the Catskill Mountains. On Saturday night, way out in the boondocks of upstate New York, three weeks early and displaying my sister's talent for unpredictability, the baby started to arrive.

I was out at a bar, Lucy's, a grungey dive with pool tables and Formica-topped furnishings in the East Village. Sasha was away so I had been flouting the whiskey ban. I had had a few shots, but I wasn't staggering thanks to the contents of the little bag of coke in my pocket.

It must have been about 1am when Euan called to tell me the baby was on its way and asked if I wanted to drive upstate to greet the new arrival.

"I can't drive," I said. "I'm drunk. Can you drive?"

"Sure," Euan said. "Get a cab over here and let's do it."

I snapped shut my phone. "Hey, Lucy," I shouted to the bar owner, then, I banged the bar and yelled, "Hey, EVERYONE!" The bar went a little quieter. "My sister's having a baby and I've got to go see it!" I put my hands in the air like a football player who had just scored a goal.

Everyone in the bar cheered. I slammed back a few more whiskey and ginger ales on the house for the road. I ducked into the bathroom and had a quick bump of coke to see me on my way.

Euan was waiting in the lobby of his building with his son Heathcliff when I got to his place in the West Village. He was piled high with toys and two car seats – one was for Alice and Floydy so they could get the baby back from the hospital.

It was a freezing October night. We got a cab out to La Guardia airport, where Hertz had a twenty-four-hour car hire depot. While Euan filled out the paperwork, I ducked into the bathroom. The cubicle was big enough to accommodate a wheelchair, brightly lit with a strip light and had pale tiles on the floor. I sat down on the toilet and took the plastic baggie out of my small jeans pocket, squeezed the ends together to open it up and worked the tip of my small mailbox key – reattached since the incident with the cops to my belt loops by its knotted green ribbon – into the powder. I raised the mound gently to my left nostril and sniffed as hard and as long as I could.

I repeated the operation another two times, then stood up, flushed the toilet for the sake and sound of appearance, and tipped my head back to inspect my nostrils in the mirror, wiping off a few telltale white crumbs. Then I went back outside to the main lobby, where I danced with Heathcliff to the Seventies classics playing on the radio while we waited for his dad to sign off on the car.

Eventually we were off, driving up the interstate towards Kingston, NY, in the dark night. I got another hit of coke when we stopped for coffee and Euan was out of the car for two minutes, and once more at the hospital.

I can't say the proudest moment of my life was frantically trying to sniff a few more grains in the hospital bathroom before I went in to see Alice, Floydy and their new daughter. I shook my head at myself in the mirror when I had finished, sighed, wiped my nose, unlocked the bathroom door and floated down the corridor to the desk where Euan was waiting for me to sign in with his little boy.

And, so, when I met Scarlet for the first time, I was wired. There was dirt under my fingernails I would never be able to shift. Scarlet was so tiny and clean and perfect and unspoiled. I was afraid to touch her. I had been like her once, I thought to myself as I bent over her clear plastic crib. Scarlet – her soft features seemed to be still forming in front of me, she was no more than two hours old – squinted blindly at the camera flashes. I felt the hot, guilty welling of tears begin behind my eyes, and wondered how Scarlet would grow up. Cocaine would be a thing of the past probably. People would shake their heads with amazement when they were told how we used to sniff powder up our noses. There'd be some new, smarter, cleaner drug to get hopped up on by the time Scarlet was eighteen. Then I realised I wasn't eighteen anymore. I was thirty, and I was high in the most profoundly inappropriate situation imaginable.

"Oh my God, Tom, you're crying," Alice said.

I just nodded, pulled a funny face and brushed the tears away.

After an hour or so at the hospital it was time to go. Euan and I bundled Heathcliff into the back of the car and we set off to find a place to stay for the night. We found a Motel 6 down the road with two double beds in one room. Euan and Heathcliff slept in one of the beds. I lay sleeplessly in the other bed for what seemed like hours, jealously watching their bodies peacefully rise and fall.

Around 7am there was a knock on the door. It was Floydy. It was whipping with freezing wind outside so he bundled in quickly.

"Hey man," I whispered, so we wouldn't wake Heathcliff up, "Congratulations. What's going on?"

"Thanks. Everyone at the hospital has gone to sleep. Can I stay here with you?" he asked.

"Yeah sure." I said, looking around the room with its two double beds. "Erm, but, you'll have to share my bed."

Floydy was red-eyed, like me.

"Oh, OK, fine," he said. He pulled off his shoes and jeans and climbed into my double bed and fell directly asleep. I waited a few moments, unsure what to do. I was wearing boxer shorts and a T-shirt, the same as Floydy. I looked around the room. Everyone was asleep. I was wired. It was a freezing, upstate, autumn morning. I climbed reluctantly into bed beside my brother-in-law, trying not to focus too hard on his stubble, or the sweaty smell of hospitals and childbirth. I lay there watching the sun come up through the blinds, panicking gently and trying to work out what, if anything, tonight meant.

-40 DAYS

MY LIFE CONTINUED to gently unravel in the weeks after Scarlet's birth. I still had my bar column at the *Post* and my one day a week at *Page Six*, but I was having more and more difficulty thinking up and writing the additional features that sustained us. I kept pulling money out of my English bank account, until one day the screen flashed up INSUFFICIENT FUNDS.

I felt sick, which was all I seemed to be feeling these days. £40,000, vaporised in two years. Where had it gone? I had drunk it, I had smoked it, I had sniffed it. I had spent my inheritance on drugs, taxis and tips. I felt blanketed in shame and stupidity.

I called Euan and asked if he could lend me $500. "No problem," he said. "When can I get it back?"

I said I didn't know. He lent me the cash anyway.

-16 DAYS

I MANAGED TO PAY our rent on December 1, 2004, but that was it. I had begged and borrowed all I could. Every time Sasha tried to talk to me about money I would play down the crisis, roll up a joint to make it go away or suggest a night out.

-7 DAYS

THE FIRST WEEKS of December passed in the familiar festive whirl of drunken parties. I had no money and no work. I got up at 3pm, sweated in the bath for an hour, stared vacantly at my computer for another hour or two or wandered into the *Post*, and then headed out to the nearest open bar. I was freezing most of the time because I wouldn't wear an overcoat to save on coat-check tips – a trick I learned from watching *The Sweet Smell of Success*. Sasha went back to England on December 9 and I couldn't even afford to pay for a car for her to the airport. She had to get the subway. I went to the station with her so I could help her with her bags.

"What are we going to do Monk?" she asked me, as we said goodbye over the turnstile.

"I dunno," I said. "I'll think of something."

But all I could think about was how much I needed a joint, a drink and a line of coke.

-6 DAYS

OR THE FIRST TIME EVER, I was glad to see Sasha go, and all the next day that realisation filled me with self-loathing and disgust. Sitting alone on my couch I shook my head, and tapped the ash off my joint into an overflowing ashtray. The apartment was disgusting. The air was fetid. It smelt of pizza and stale smoke but it was too cold to open the window. The filth didn't really bother me, and if I did clean the place up it was only going to get messed up again, so what would be the point?

I tried to analyse my feelings of relief that Sasha had gone. Why was I glad? Was it because the leash was off? Because I could stay out as late as I wanted? Because I wouldn't have to sneak up to the roof for my mid-morning joint?

It all sounded logical, but the problem was that none of that really made any sense. Sasha hadn't ever chastised me about my drinking. She loved a party. Sometimes she would drink more than me. I knew from our late-night chats that when we first got together one of the things that had attracted her to me was my drinking prowess. She had told me, "I used to find it embarrassing when I went on dates with guys and they couldn't drink as much as me." She never had that problem with me.

Yet somehow a tremendous distance had opened up between us. I was miles and miles away from the shore now.

I upset the ashtray, suddenly furious with Sasha for abandoning me. But what did I expect her to do? She'd already made it clear she wasn't going to play the part of the nagging wife. She had suggested I try cutting down. I had tried, and I had failed. I wanted to drink.

Maybe the reason she never confronted me about my drinking was because she hoped, like me, that if she ignored the problem long enough it would resolve itself, melt away. Maybe she was telling herself, like I was, that it wasn't so bad. That it was just a phase. That everything would be alright in the end. That we were normal.

Late that evening, when I got into bed, I finally realised why I wanted to be alone. It was because I didn't have to invent an excuse – to myself or to Sasha – why I didn't want to have sex. Over the last year when we were lying next to each other in bed, I had taken to feigning sleep to avoid physical intimacy. Well, I realised, it was either that, or stay out all night and sleep on the sofa, which more or less amounted to the same thing.

We were doomed. How would we ever be able to raise a child? Where would we live? Who would employ me? How long would it be until I was found out at the *Post* and fired again?

The thoughts cycled through my head as I lay there in the darkness, so I got out of bed, went back through to the sitting room and flicked on the television. A beer and a joint were all the company I needed.

At least they made me feel better.

23

-3 DAYS

IT WAS WEDNESDAY night and a big, ounce bag of weed was bulging in my pocket, and Chris and I, having finished work ten minutes previously, were picking up a dozen beers from the deli on the corner of his block before heading back to his place for a smoke to get the night started.

Chris's skinny midtown apartment was a den of bachelor iniquity. There was trash everywhere, empty beer cans on the table and a weed pipe on the sideboard. Two massive works by Peter Tunney hung on the wall – a gift from the artist. In Chris's bedroom there was an enormous cardboard box filled with feminine fripperies – cosmetics, underwear, fragrance.

"What's this stuff?" I asked him, peering through the doorway.

"That's like my personal goody bag supply," Chris said. "It's all the girly shit I get sent at work. I always tell girls who stay over to grab something from it when they leave in the morning."

I sat on the sofa and pulled the bag of marijuana out of my pocket, and set about rolling up a joint.

I took a few hits and then passed it to Chris, exhaling as I sat back in the sofa. We passed it back and forth, and when the joint was finished I started piecing together the papers for another one.

I lit it but Chris declined to smoke any more. "No way man, I'm done," he said, and we sat there in silence for a bit.

Then Chris pulled out a DVD and said, "But if you want to get high, then we should watch this."

I looked at the case as Chris loaded the DVD. It was a film called, *How's Your News?* and it was a documentary about a team of mentally and physically disabled people travelling around the country as a news team. One guy, a dwarf, had a deliberately over-sized microphone with a huge question mark scrawled on it to make himself look even freakier than he already did. I couldn't work out who I was supposed to be identifying with.

After an hour or so, we gathered up our things to head out. No need to discuss where we were going. On a night like this, in a state like this, there was only one option: Siberia.

It was raining, and my feet slapped heavily against the wet pavement as we hurried down 9th Avenue. When I pushed open the door and walked into the bar, Tracey gave me and Chris a hug and demanded to know what we wanted.

Sitting at the bar, I regretted getting so stoned before going out. I wasn't good for much now. I couldn't really get interested in any of the conversations in the bar, and I was zoning in and out.

Fortunately, I knew a way to break out of my viscous, stoned bubble. "Patrick," I called down the bar, "Can I get a martini please?"

The mathematics of cross-substance inebriation are a complex business. Getting stoned makes you sleepy, but a few drinks wake you up. The only problem is that the drinks eventually catch up with you and make you sloppy. That's when you need stimulants.

By the time I had put away two more martinis, I needed stimulation. I called a dealer's pager number, entered my phone number after the beeps, and twenty minutes later the guy called me from outside Siberia. I went out, climbed in his car, and he said, "Hi – one?"

I nodded, he handed me a bag of cocaine, I passed him a $50 bill and then he was gone.

Half an hour later I was buzzing. Chris was laughing, I was laughing, and I was telling him something important.

"The thing is man, I always felt like you were my soul mate. And it's not just the booze, or the partying. It's just that ... you get it, man. You get it. I love you brother. You're a merchant after my own soul. Man, one of these days we'll have to go to rehab together, but until then, man, you know, let's just rip it up and party."

Chris was pretty wasted as well, but not that wasted. He had scowled under his beard when I joked about rehab. "Rehab man? No way. We're not that bad. At least, *I'm* not."

I shrugged, reached into my pocket to get my cocaine, but my fingertips touched something big and square. I pulled it out and looked at it quizzically. It was the new Ozzy Osbourne greatest hits CD, *The Ozman Cometh*. I'd been sent it at work. I put it on the bar. I wondered whether Patrick would put it on for me?

I loved that tune *Paranoid*.

I picked up my martini and took a glug. It seemed a bit weak.

"Patrick," I called out over the long wooden bar, "Did you let the ice melt in this or something?"

And then everything went blank.

24

-2 DAYS

i WOKE UP the next morning remembering nothing, feeling just panic and pain.

Judging by my hangover, it had been quite a night. Whatever I had done – and I was pretty certain I had done *something* – it had obviously involved a prodigious quantity of alcohol. I had a monstrous, seething, abomination of a hangover. I tried to lie still because my head hurt whenever I moved it, my dehydrated brain bruising as it banged against the sides of my skull.

"What did I do last night?" I groaned, out loud, to myself.

Fortunately, I was a master of hangover cures. The most effective hangover cure is to simply drink three pints of water before you get into bed. It's also the hardest to pull off, as the drunkard's appetite for water is reduced in direct ratio to the amount of alcohol consumed. When you have a couple of pints of liquor working their way through your system, the prospect of chugging water for half an hour is not appealing.

So I hadn't drunk my water. Nor had I vomited before going to bed, swallowed any Tylenol before retiring, or even eaten a big, greasy serving of street meat. Even though Sasha was away, I had still crashed out on my battered and stained sofa of shame. I had woken there in the early morning and staggered through to the bedroom in the putrid half-light. Now, awake for the second time, I realised I was still dressed in last night's clothes.

I tried to think rationally. I rolled gingerly out of bed and ran a boiling hot bath, a real lobster-boiler, and cautiously lowered myself into it. Once my body had got used to the scalding temperature, I nudged the hot tap on again with my big toe. I let it run for a few seconds until the temperature was unbearable and then shut it off. A few minutes later, when I was acclimatised, I gave the faucet another nudge with my toe, raising the temperature a few more degrees, sweating out my hangover.

Man, did I feel bad. I groaned out loud. The night was a blank but I tried to piece it together. I remembered going to Chris's house after work and watching that bizarre video, then, I thought, we had gone to Siberia. I simply couldn't remember anything else.

Eventually I got out of the bathtub and shaved, wiping the condensation off the mirror with every swipe of the razor. I thought I was going to faint. I went back to my bedroom and lay down on the covers to cool off. After twenty minutes, when I had finished actually steaming, I put on a shirt and my Kilgour suit. I checked my appearance in the mirror. I no longer looked like a hungover reprobate. I looked more like a successful – if somewhat pale – nightlife professional.

Walking down 6th Avenue, I had a bleary flashback to pretending to be a pinball on this street the night before. What the hell had that been about? I shook my head at my foolish antics and snickered out loud at the half-memory. I was still kind of wasted. I felt a little dizzy and touched my head and face. It seemed like they were distorted, out of shape somehow.

I walked into the lobby of the *Post* building shortly before 5pm. It was getting dark. Just another busy day in the life of a bar columnist, right? I took the elevator up to the tenth floor, and walked to my desk in the features department.

"Hey," said my friend Elysa Lipsky-Karasz, who sat at the desk opposite me. "What's going on? Why are you looking so smart?"

What could I say? *Because I just got out of bed and I am trying to hide how hungover I am.* Probably not a good idea. I made up an instant lie instead. "Oh, I just had some meetings and stuff to do today," I said. Then I added, "You know, job interviews, that kind of stuff."

"Really?" said Elysa.

I rolled my eyes and gave her the "Shh" sign. It seemed

to work. After ten minutes it was like I had been there all day. Same stupid emails, I thought as I deleted my way through them. But one caught my eye. It was titled, "Dinner for fifteen tonight?"

Huh? I opened it up.

"Tom, just checking you still want a table for fifteen tonight at the opening of Jeffrey Chodorow's new restaurant Caviar and Banana. We have reserved you the private room, and we are wrapping all the Brazilian knick-knacks in bubble-wrap in anticipation of your arrival. See you later. Patricia."

Oh shit. I had completely forgotten that I had planned this – the biggest freebie ever, for fifteen people. And we had a private room as well.

"Hey, Elysa," I called over. "Are you still on for this dinner tonight?"

"Yeah, sure, I'm coming," she said.

I made a few other calls. Everyone seemed to be on for it. I desperately wanted to back out, go home and curl up in a ball in front of the television and try not to drink. But there was no way out of this now. I'd have to go. Anyway, I'd probably feel OK after a few cocktails, I reasoned. I emailed the PR. "We'll be there. Nice of you to clear the area. Tom."

She sent back a smiley face. I felt sick.

I'd invited Chris and Paula as well so I thought I'd wander round to their desks and see whether they were still up for it. I walked round to *Page Six* and leaned over the giant black filing cabinet that formed the back wall of their cubicles.

"Yo!" I said. "What's up? You guys still on for tonight?"

Chris looked up at me with a massive grin. "Oh my god," he said with relish, "Look at you, man! Smart! Nobody would ever know!"

I started to feel the heat build in my cheeks. I looked around uncomfortably, as if he was talking to someone else.

"What man?" I asked. "What do you mean?"

"I mean last night man!"

"What?" I said, shrugging with the palms of my hands. "What about last night?"

Chris smiled as he realised I couldn't remember. "Don't tell me you can't remember what you did last night?" he laughed. "Oh my Lord!"

"Yeah man, I remember," I said, starting to sweat, starting to feel unsure. "We went back to yours, watched that DVD, and then we went to Siberia."

"Yes, and then ..."

"What man?" I said, getting redder and redder and hotter and hotter and hotter. "What?" Paula and Richard were both looking at me with half-smiles now. *They* had already been told what I did. I sighed. "OK. What the fuck *did* I do last night?" I almost shouted it.

"Dude," said Chris, with relish, "*You smashed up the fucking Pac-Man!*"

All the blood in my body churned through my ears with a huge, noisy whoosh and BANG, it all came back to me.

I gasped and then swallowed hard. I remembered being Ozzy, the lights in my eyes, singing along. The glass sparkling on the chair legs. And then looking down on myself. Tracey bear-hugging me off the stage.

My head was spinning. Shit. This was not good. Richard Johnson, the editor of *Page Six*, my boss one day a week for Christ's sake, was looking at me dubiously.

The self-defence mechanism kicked in. *Laugh it off. Say the right thing and it'll all be OK.*

So I said, "Oh *that*. I was, you know, just trying to raise the tone of Siberia a little bit."

Silence.

"Anyway," I said, rubbing my hands with a little too much enthusiasm. "Are you guys still on for tonight?"

I was always on for another night.

At the restaurant that night I cornered Chris.

"Is Tracey pissed with me?"

"Oh, I doubt he even cares," said Chris. "I mean, it's Siberia, you know. It'll just become another one of the legends. 'The night Tom Sykes smashed up the Pac Man'. Don't worry about it."

"Yeah, I guess," I said, unconvinced.

Chris took a sip of his wine. "Seriously, Tracey won't give a shit, man. Did you ever hear about the night of the thousand shattering glasses?"

"No," I said.

"There have been a couple of them actually. It's when we just smash up and destroy every single bottle, every glass, every mirror, everything in the whole bar. And like, you know, Tracey joins in. Tracey fucking *starts* it man.

Everything! All the spirits, all the beers, everything, we just smash everything up."

At that moment, Jeffrey Chodorow, the owner of the new restaurant, walked up to me, glaring, and said, "Hey, Tom. Sorry if this place is a bit, uh, 'soulless' for you," and stalked off.

"What was that about?" Chris asked me, confused.

"Oh, I put this item in *Page Six* that Anthony Bourdain said his restaurants were 'soulless'. So I guess he's pissed about that."

"You wrote that his restaurants were soulless then over-took the private room for a party on the opening night?" Chris is laughing again. I'm not.

I feel sick again, dizzy from the conflation of a hangover and caipirinhias.

We sat down to dinner in a large, bare room, that had indeed been denuded of all ornamentation. I overheard Chris say to the person on my left, "So, you'll never guess what happened to me and Tom last night?"

I shivered, wondering if this was where my luck would finally run out. I'd got away with a lot of nonsense in my time but this was different. I'd smashed up a bar, for god's sake. Violence, even against an inanimate object, well, that was a new and unwelcome line that had been crossed.

The chatter around the table was lively and loud, but I wasn't a part of it. I was zoning out, staring at a wine bottle on the table.

Distantly, I became aware of Elysa shouting, "Tom! Tom!"

I snapped out of my trance, trying to smile, trying to hold it together.

"What?" I said.

"My god, you were miles away," said Elysa. "Are you going out after this?"

"Er, I dunno," I said. I should have gone home. I wanted to go home. But I didn't. At 4am I was staggering home, glad there were still a few hours to sunrise.

Tomorrow was Friday. *Page Six* day. I drank my water that night, and got into my bed not the sofa. I shut my eyes to go to sleep, but I started spinning.

I was back in Siberia, twenty feet up in the air on a 35-degree angle looking down at myself beating the crap out of the Pac-Man again.

SMASH! *Who is that person?*

SMASH! *That can't be me.*

SMASH! *What have I become?*

25

-1 DAY

Somehow I got through that Friday at the office. My head pounded. My eyes, my kidneys, my nose – my whole body ached. I had a metal band around my chest, cramps in my bladder and shooting pains in my bowel. When I went to the bathroom, my shit was full of blood. That wasn't so unusual, to be honest, but that Friday, sitting on the toilet, staring at the bloody piece of toilet roll in my hand, I longed desperately to be well.

I kept knocking back painkillers but they had no effect. The day dragged on forever. I had a sick feeling in my stomach. I kept trying to convince myself it was hunger but when I was in the bathroom and retched, I could taste the bitter alcoholic leftovers in my bile. Even worse, I could taste shame.

I needed a quiet night in. I would have gone to see a movie with Sasha, but she was still in Ireland. Usually, when

Sasha was away, we would speak every day, but since I had smashed up Siberia on Wednesday night I had been avoiding her calls, just sending her vague text messages from my mobile phone. I didn't want to scare her.

Late in the afternoon I rang my sister Alice and invited myself to her place for dinner. Then I went outside. After walking twice around the block, and smoking a couple of cigarettes, I took a deep breath and pulled out my phone. On a piece of paper in my pocket, I had scrawled the number of my health insurance company.

With the aid of several deep breaths I dialled the number. The person on the other end of the phone asked how they could help.

I screwed my eyes up tight and asked, "Am I covered for rehabilitation from alcohol?"

I spent ten minutes on the phone, being passed between various departments. I ended up at mental health. Although I walked farther and farther away from the office, I frequently had to drop my voice because I kept passing work colleagues on the street, and I didn't want them to hear any telltale snippets of my conversation.

"Do you want to make an appointment for an assessment?" a guy on the other end of the phone eventually asked me.

Was I really having this conversation? What was I doing? I tilted my head up and looked at the freezing blue winter sky. Sure, I drank a bit too much, and sometimes I even shat blood, but that was no reason to panic.

"No," I replied, "I'm just asking." I hung up, snapped my phone shut, and went back into the office. I wasn't that bad, was I?

After work, I picked up a bottle of wine on my way to Alice's apartment. It was warm and cosy in her apartment and her baby Scarlet, a little over six weeks old, was fast asleep in her crib. We had to keep our voices down. I opened the bottle of wine and poured us both a glass. Alice took one sip and grimaced.

"Yuk," she said. "It's weird, I haven't really got back into drinking since I had Scarlet. I just don't feel like it."

I was already halfway through my glass, "Good," I said. "All the more for me."

Alice cooked some sausages, mashed potatoes and baked beans for our dinner and we watched a bit of television. I felt safe and protected in her apartment, with Scarlet gurgling gently in her cot.

I offered to clear away the plates, refilling my glass for the third time in the kitchen. The bottle was almost done. I gulped back my glass, then just poured out the rest of the bottle.

"So, what's been going on?" Alice asked me, as I sat back down on the sofa with my glass of wine.

"Well," I said, laughing, "I went crazy the other night in Siberia and smashed the place up."

Alice didn't laugh. She looked at me, horrified, and grabbed a hand to her throat. Her whole face went red.

"*What?*" she said, whispering it too loud. Scarlet gave a

little squeak. Then quieter, but with the same urgency, she said, "*Tom*, what do you mean?"

"Oh, it's nothing," I said.

I told her the whole story. Well, almost the whole story. I left out the bit about the out-of-body experience. I didn't want to freak her out.

Alice just stared at me.

"Tom," she said, finally, "What are you going to do?"

"Well," I said, "I don't know. Just try and cut down a bit I guess." There was a long silence. I swallowed hard, looked at my feet.

"But Tom, haven't you been trying to cut down?"

"Yes."

Another silence. So I said, "Actually, I phoned my health insurance people and they said I was eligible for rehab. I could go in for thirty days. You know, quit."

I thought she'd say, "Oh, well, I think that's a bit extreme," or, "Don't be silly."

But her eyes lit up. And she said, "Oh my God, Tom, that would be brilliant."

Maybe I *was* that bad after all.

26

-1 DAY (CONTINUED)

i LEFT ALICE'S HOUSE, got out of the subway at 55th Street and started walking back to my apartment through crowds of drunken revellers careening around midtown, trying out the word "rehab" on my tongue. It didn't sound right. I felt fine now, anyway.

I hate December. Christmas is the worst time of year for the serious drinker. The bars and clubs are full of idiots in suits who can't take their drink, being sick on the street after three vodka and tonics. Amateur hour.

I saw Jean from La Bonne Soupe standing outside the restaurant having a smoke.

"All right Jean," I said, mooching up to him and shaking hands. "How's it going?"

"My God, it has been like a zoo in there," he said, sighing and nodding to the restaurant. "There has been a line outside since 4pm. It's totally insane." He looked exhausted. "How are you doing?"

"Pretty good," I said. "Missing Sasha."

"Sasha is in Ireland still?" asked Jean. "When is she getting back?"

"Next Thursday or Friday, I think, then we are staying in New York for Christmas."

"Are you going tonight?" asked Jean.

"Going where?" I said.

"To the party! There is a Christmas party at the bar across the road for all the staff at the restaurant."

I'd forgotten all about it. Yves, who owned La Bonne Soupe, had invited me to the staff party earlier in the week. I shouldn't go really, I should go home, but Yves would be disappointed if I didn't show my face. And Yves always had terrific wine at his parties. "It's going on now?" I asked.

"Yes," said Jean. "Right across the street."

I told Jean I would see him there later, spun on my heel and walked over. There was no way I was going to go to rehab. I wasn't that bad. I said out loud, "I blame Christmas!" and laughed out loud at myself.

The party was jammed with beautiful French girls and cool French boys drinking wine and dancing to Euro pop music. I grabbed a glass and started chatting to some of the staff from the restaurant. Someone handed me a package of coke and I went into the bathroom and poured out a fat line for myself on the toilet cistern. Then I went back to the party and drank more.

The next thing I knew I was surrounded by four angry Italian–American guys.

"You wanna get fucked up?" one of them was saying. "You wanna get fucked up just carry on talking you prick." He was jabbing me in the chest with his finger. "You wanna get fucked up?"

"No," I said, "I don't wanna get fucked up." What the hell was going on? How did I get into this? I had no idea. I must have lost an hour or two somewhere.

"Then just shut up and get the hell out of here," another one was shouting. "Can you do that? Can you just get out of here?" He was thrusting my copy of *The Ozman Cometh* into my jacket pocket. I looked at it confused.

"And take your music with you."

Uh-oh. Ozzy must have been getting me into trouble again.

"Sure," I said, "I mean, I guess I could …"

I tottered backwards on my feet as the guy punched me on my cheekbone.

"Get out of here now!" he was screaming.

For once I was smart enough to not say anything. I just headed for the door, down the stairs, across the road and back to my house, my cheek throbbing. I had no idea what I had done. What did I do? I pulled myself up the stairs to my apartment by the banister.

Inside, I yanked open the fridge door, grabbed three beers that were in there, and heaved open the freezer, retrieving a quarter-full bottle of Stolichnaya.

I sat down heavily on the sofa and felt something in the back pocket of my jeans crack under my weight. I shoved my hand down and pulled out the Ozzy Osbourne CD, now with a split across the plastic casing. I tried to get up to put it on but I staggered, lost my balance and crashed back down on the sofa. On the third try I made it.

I knew it was late, but I was surprised when the night started to break into another ghastly day as Ozzy kicked off again. I drank my beers. I pulled out my bag of weed and poured all the dry, crumbly herb into a rolling paper to make one last joint.

I poured the vodka into a tumbler. Ozzy was singing *Goodbye to Romance.*

Sitting on the sofa at 5am with another grey day breaking, surrounded by beer cans and despair, I didn't know what to do any more. A tear rolled down my cheek.

"This has to stop," I mumbled, as I pulled one last time on the joint, burning my fingers and stubbing it out in the overflowing ashtray.

"This has to stop," I muttered, as I drained the glass of vodka, feeling the familiar burn of alcohol in my throat.

"This has to *stop*," I whispered, as I got up, hit the power button on the CD player, shuffled into my bedroom, wiped the tears from my face and collapsed gratefully into oblivion.

27

DAY ZERO

i JOLTED AWAKE some time on Saturday afternoon, and before I had time to register my savage hangover or talk myself out of it I scrabbled for my phone and called my health insurance company again.

"I think I need to go to rehab for alcohol addiction," I said, when a person answered. It was a relief to finally say it.

I got funnelled through the various departments again, but eventually I spoke to a man who explained that it would take at least a week to get admitted somewhere.

I couldn't do another week, I told him, and hung up, grabbed my laptop and typed "alcohol addiction quit" into Google, and called the first number that came up.

A gruff Brooklyn voice answered, "Yeah?"

At that moment all I wanted to do was hang up. I wanted to say, "I'm sorry! Wrong number. I'm just fine! All I need is a cocktail."

Instead, I managed to say, "I need help."

The gruff guy told me that I needed to get to a "meeting", and gave me some directions to the nearest one.

I was willing to try anything, so, half an hour later, bundled up against the cold, I stood outside a faceless office building in Times Square. A few dozen yards away, way above my head, on a screen the size of a football field, a giant bottle of vodka levitated, spun, and slowly filled up a beaded martini glass. I wanted to reach out and touch it. Yellow cabs flew by me in a blur of lights and horns on every side. A mariachi band was striking up a tune. Tourists and hustlers bumped past me. It felt like someone was playing a movie in slow motion.

You could hail a cab right now, be downtown in a bar in ten minutes.

But I didn't have any money. I turned my gaze away from the massive martini, and bundled in to the anonymous building with a gust of freezing air.

A security guard sat by the elevator. He looked up from his newspaper and shot me a thin smile as I pushed the door open. He *knew*.

I took the creaky, piss-smelling elevator up to the third floor and wandered down a deserted hallway to a locked door. A scribbled note on it gave a number to page, "If no one shows up."

Great. These people, who were supposed to get me sober, couldn't even manage to unlock a door. I dialled the number, and keyed in my digits at the beep. It felt uncannily like calling my drug dealer.

And then I just stood there, waiting for the phone to ring, trying not to listen to a voice in my head, that was saying, *"What are you doing? There's nothing wrong with you. You're not that bad. You just need to tone it down a bit. Turn around now. It's not too late to pretend none of this ever happened."*

Twenty minutes later, bloodshot and shot to pieces, I took a seat in a hard chair the colour of shit in a circle of hard chairs the colour of shit in a gloomy room made more depressing by futile attempts to brighten it up. Christmas lights. A brightly coloured neon clock. God help me.

The seven or so other self-professed alcoholics in the room kept falling asleep – but they got excited when I introduced myself.

"Hi. I'm Tom. I guess I'm an alcoholic. And this is my first meeting ever."

The meeting freaked me out. One guy had obviously drunk so much that he had burned out his stomach. He burped constantly. Another man with a beard, bright eyes, long hair and tiny sparrow-like features said, "Welcome!" Then he told me he choreographed modern dance. Would I like to come to a performance sometime?

Another guy talked about God. His grace. His will. His power. Had I wandered into a cult? I realised I didn't really care if I had. I was so desperate, so bereft, I would have painted a spot on my head if I thought it would help me feel better.

After an hour they all stood up, linked hands, grabbed mine, and said a prayer.

"God, grant me the serenity to accept the things I cannot change, the courage to change the things I can and the wisdom to tell the difference."

Before I could make it out of the door they were on me, pouncing like missionaries. They thrust books in my hands. They gave me cards with their phone numbers, which I threw in the bin as soon as I got out of sight.

One guy, with a pink scarf and two plastic carrier bags said, "Call me anytime. I stay up late, late, late."

I said, "OK! See you!"

The bearded dance choreographer with the bright eyes said one thing that made sense. I had to "count days" until I got ninety days clean and sober. That seemed like a reasonable objective, I thought to myself as I began walking home. Three months off the booze and I'd be OK to drink again.

My route home took me through the middle of Times Square again. The giant vodka advertisement had been replaced by a giant Budweiser advertisement. My phone rang. It was Sasha. I let it go to voicemail. Sasha had called three times today already, her messages increasingly feverish and concerned.

This one was no different. "Where are you Monk? Are you alright? I haven't spoken to you in three days, why aren't you calling me back?"

I didn't call her back because if I failed, I didn't want anyone, not even my wife, to know I had tried.

The eighty-foot sign bleached out my phone as it flashed the message "KING OF BEERS" around Times Square.

DAYS 1-4

T HE FIRST DAYS of withdrawing from alcohol were absolutely agonising, indescribably awful. Sleep without vodka was impossible. A sympathetic friend gave me a few sleeping pills, but they hardly worked. I had to sleep in my bathrobe because I sweated so much at night I kept thinking I had pissed the bed.

On day two I sat at my computer screen in my bedroom trying to write about what was going on, when I saw the black shadow of a rat run across the floor. I leapt up in a panic, and gingerly lifted up the old towels and clothes strewn across the floor, but there was nothing there. I sat back down. A few minutes later, the rat ran past the corner of my eye again.

"You're imagining it," I said to myself. Then little black bugs started to scuttle across the white walls.

I checked the web to see what was going on and found my answer: "Alcohol hallucinosis," I read. "This symptom usually begins twelve to twenty-four hours after your last drink, and may last as long as two days once it begins. It is common for people who are withdrawing from alcohol to see multiple, small, similar moving objects. Sometimes the vision is perceived to be crawling insects."

That night I lay in bed and shut my eyes but the hallucinations found a way through. Sudden, loud noises like someone was beating a drum in my ear forced me upright in the night, sweaty, swallowing hard and staring, desperately searching for the light switch.

On day four I took a good look around my apartment. The place was still drunk. Alcohol containers were strewn across the floor, overflowing out of the bin, littered under the bed. The washing-up in the sink was alive. A thin film of filth covered everything. I had to tidy up.

The worst part was finding all the half-empty bottles of alcohol. It was like the end of a party when all that's left is the seriously gross stuff – green Apple Pucker, Blue Curacao, fruit liqueur, even some Slivovitch from a trip to Eastern Europe. I poured one after the other down the sink in a trance, my mouth watering as I smelt the fumes.

In an ashtray I found an old joint. The paper holding it together was stained brown with tar that had coalesced where the paper had been licked down. And I thought, well, what the hell.

I looked for a light but I couldn't find one, so I fired up the gas hob. I lit the joint, and pulled back from the gas when I heard a crackle and smelt my hair burning. I inhaled deeply on the joint, holding the smoke in my lungs until I thought I was going to burst. Then, ahhh, exhale.

I got maybe five puffs out of the joint. When I stubbed it out the first thing I thought was "*I'd kill for a drink.*"

I sat down on the sofa, sitting on my hands, but the craving kept coming at me.

This is all a mistake. I'm not an alcoholic. And if I am I don't care. I'm not like those other bums. I don't drink vodka outside the Port Authority. I drink Dirty Martinis at Bungalow 8. I'm different. I'm a writer. I'm supposed to be a drunk. Did Hemingway ever quit? Or Bukowski, for god's sake?"

I got up and headed for the door. I'm going to go and get drunk, I thought. As I was walking out of the door I decided to call one of the numbers I had been given to let them know I was giving up giving up. I talked about smoking the joint with the man who answered. I told him I was about to go and get drunk.

He said, "You're doing so well, though. You just need to wait till the joint wears off. Three hours maximum."

How did he know about the three hours thing?

"Can you hold out for three hours?" the guy said. "If you still want a drink in three hours I won't try and talk you out of it. Do you want me to come round?"

No, thank you very fucking much, I don't want you to come round you pathetic freak. Don't you have anything better to do with your sad and lonely life?

"No, you don't need to come round," I said. "I'll give it three hours."

I continued manically cleaning my apartment for the next three hours, and in an old file I found a gold pocket watch my dad had given me for my wedding present. I thought I had lost it. I stared at the watch for twenty minutes and thought about my dad. I wanted to cry, but I couldn't. All my emotions seemed to have been cauterised.

The guy rang back.

"Hey, Tom, how's it going? Still want a drink?"

"No," I said. "Do I have to start counting days again?" I asked.

"Up to you," he says. "Some people would say no, this is just about alcohol. If you want my opinion, I think you should. My opinion is that you can't be high and sober at the same time, but that's just me."

"But if I have to start counting days again, then why didn't I just go and get drunk?" I shouted, furious as I realised what I have been denied – for *nothing*.

"Do you want to be drunk now?" he asked me.

"No," I said. "I don't want to be drunk now."

Silence.

"I'll start counting days again," I said.

"OK," he said.

I was angry when I hung up. I felt like a child. I got into bed and lay there, just watching the digits on the clock advance towards meeting time, 10.30pm. I went to the meeting that night and said, "I have today. Well, this afternoon. A couple of hours really. I smoked a joint." I paused, and then said furiously, "I had *four days*. I can't believe I have got to start counting days again."

The room exploded into laughter, and for a few seconds I burnt with embarrassment and hatred and rage. Then I started to laugh as well, big huge, gasping laughs that sounded more like sobs, and slowly but surely turned into them.

28

DAY 1 REDUX

i EVENTUALLY PICKED UP the phone when Sasha rang for the third time on my second first day. She was due back in New York the following day anyway, and I thought it might be best if she had twenty-four hours to take in the news.

She said, "Monk, where have you been? Why haven't you called me back?"

I replied, "Er, I've got something to tell you."

"What?" she demanded. "What is it? What's going on?"

I began to blush and feel stupid. *I don't want to be boring.* I felt like I was betraying myself and my marriage and everything I ever stood for when I said, "I've quit drinking."

"Oh my god, what happened?" she asked.

And so I tell her. I tell her about the Pac-Man machine. I remind her about the money running out. I don't tell her about getting punched, but I do tell her about the despair.

My hands look thin and frail as I talk. I have turned from red to pink to translucent white and finally to a ghastly green. I feel green inside.

"Oh my god," says Sasha again. She sounds totally freaked out. Her voice is thin and frightened. I can't tell whether she's scared by the stories or the stopping-drinking part.

There's silence for a few seconds, then Sasha says, "I feel so guilty not being there to support you. I'm going to get on a plane now and come back tonight. I don't care what it costs."

"No," I say, "Don't. You don't need to do that. I think it's good I did this while you were away anyway. I can't wait for you to get back, Sash, but I think this is something I have to do myself. It's a solo mission."

Sitting on the sofa watching a DVD the next afternoon, just trying to get through the day, wondering how Sasha is going to handle it and how I will get through Christmas, my hands wander over my shoulder to feel my back. It is covered in boils – angry, painful swellings, rooted deep below the surface of my skin. Although they hurt to touch, I can't stop prodding and pushing them, forcing them to the surface. I run a bath and sit in it for hours trying to squeeze them. Eventually one bursts, with an orgasmic, evil burst of pure pain. I inspect the sticky, yellow goo on my fingers. Even from a distance, it stinks of sourness and decay. I am disgusting, but I console myself with the unrealistic hope that maybe my body is beginning to expel some of the toxins that have accumulated over the years.

Sasha arrives back late that night. I run down the stairs when she buzzes, kiss her and carry her suitcase up the stairs. I am trying to look caring, responsible, in control, considerate, like I am getting better. In fact, the effort just exposes how sick I am – despite the freezing cold night the exertion soaks my T-shirt with foul-smelling sweat.

Sasha wants to talk but I don't know what to tell her. I try to fill the time with activity instead. I go across the road and get some soups to take away.

We sit down to eat and I can't put off the conversation any more.

Sasha says, "I think it's really amazing what you are doing."

I squirm uncomfortably, afraid I am not going to make it, even to ninety days.

"Are you freaked out?" I ask.

"No," she says, smiling, holding my clammy hand. I can tell she's lying. Of course she's freaked out. She's probably thinking some of the same things I am thinking. Is our life over? Can I do this? Am I going to be boring from now on? Are we ever going to have fun again? And worst of all, what happens if I don't make it? Do I die? Is that the endgame?

Neither of us knows the answers.

"I'm going to go out in a bit," I say. "I'm going to go to a meeting."

I spend the next week sitting up late in a diner with some of the crazy people I have met in the meetings. I stay out late, just eating, eating, eating. I know Sasha is at home, confused, baffled, scared, but I can't go back there right now. I have to eat.

One guy tells me that when he got sober he ate three Indian take-outs a night every night for two weeks. He is thinner than David Bowie. "Just do what your body tells you," he says. I reflect that I have hardly eaten at all for the past five years. Maybe my body is playing catch-up. I don't know anymore.

Basically, I feel like death. I know just how much trouble I am in when I get home that night, climb into bed and Sasha tells me, in all seriousness, that I look better than I have done for years. "I'm so proud of you," she whispers. "I'm so excited about the rest of our lives together."

I am consumed with dread that I won't make it.

DAY 12

CHRISTMAS COMES and goes. It's like it's happening somewhere else. My mum visits New York and we have lunch. We go for a walk down the river, and I just tell her, "I'm not drinking."

She starts telling me what a good thing that is because of all the sugars alcohol contains. I feel angry but I don't want to get into it. I say, "Mum, it's not the sugars. It's the alcohol."

I keep going back to the meetings because I love the applause. I stick my hand in the air and holler, "Hi. My

name is Tom and I am an alcoholic. I have twelve days."
Applause. Cries of "Keep coming back". I sit rocking on my
chair, trying not to think, just letting my mind run.

I lie sleeplessly in bed, until eventually I turn on the
light and scribble on a piece of paper, "If I don't drink, who
will I be?"

I don't have any answers.

DAY 40

I FEEL GOOD. My skin looks great. The boils are going. In
fact, it's hard to believe I ever had a problem at all. *Maybe
I am not an alcoholic. Maybe I made it all up. I'd love a drink.*

I do the maths to keep myself focused. The first five or
six years of my drinking, from age fourteen to nineteen or
twenty, I probably averaged about four drinks a night, maybe
a total of some seven thousand drinks. The last ten years of
my drinking, maybe ten a night. Is that fifty thousand drinks?
I could work it out, but really, it means nothing to me.

Over the next few weeks, dramatic improvement gives
way to steady progress. I wake up in the mornings without
a hangover, for example. I feel like I am writing better
than I ever have in my life – although I don't have much
work. I had to go into the *Post* to tell Faye about my little
problem and explain that my days as a nightlife writer are
well and truly over.

Faye's amazing. She wishes me good luck. She tells me that newspapers are full of raging alcoholics. She tells me she'll find me other work at the paper. She says, "I didn't know you had a problem with alcohol, but it figures. It makes sense."

"Why?" I ask.

"Well, your work was always so inconsistent. Sometimes it was terrific, sometimes it was just a mess."

I nod my head sadly.

I don't drink and I go to meetings, two, even three a day. It helps to be around people who have been through what I am going through and much, much worse.

One guy took so much cocaine he thought he had bugs under his skin and cut open his shoulder to get them out. Another guy was in the Iraq War where he got hooked on prescription drugs they called "combat cocktails". His two best friends got their heads blown off while they were standing next to him. There's a woman who spent years in destitution collecting empty bottles and cardboard in Bolivia to pay for moonshine. Another lady slept in old refrigerators. A musician reminisces how he could never have less than $6,000 of heroin in his possession at all times. "Just in case," he explains, and we all nod.

But as I start to feel better, it gets complicated, because I want my life back. I don't want to drink, but I do want to see some of my friends. And now I was going to do just that.

Four of the guys – James, my old dealer, Olly, my best man, my mate Frank and Tom Craig, the photographer I lived with in London after university – arrive in New York for a reunion planned long before my decision to quit. I manage one cranberry-juice-fuelled night out in New York, but the next morning Sasha and I pile them all in the back of a Mercedes G-Wagon and drive to Vermont for a few days skiing.

They are so hungover that the whole car stinks of booze. They have hardly been to sleep. I feel *so* jealous.

One night they want to go to the pub, so I drive them a mile or so up the road, go back to our apartment with Sasha, and pick them up at midnight. I feel like my mother.

On the last run of the last day, I sit on the ski lift with Tom. I congratulate him on how well his career is going. He turns to me, the snow whipping across our faces and says, "I think what you're doing is so fantastic. It's a real lesson in getting the most out of your life. I'm proud of you, big man."

I pull my goggles down so he can't see my tears.

But still that little voice, telling me that maybe, maybe it would be OK. Just one last time.

DAY 90

I GET NINETY DAYS clean and sober. I invite my sisters and some friends round for a little party. Sasha bakes a choco-late cake. She decorates it with M&Ms spelling ninety!

The first surreal moment comes when my friend Vivien, who I haven't seen for a year, calls, quite by chance, to say he has just landed in New York from Australia. Come round, I say, I'm having a sober party.

"You *what*?"

"I'll explain when you get here."

Then, *another* friend, Piers, who I have not seen in maybe two years, calls. Randomly, *he* has just landed in New York from London. Come round, I say, I'm having a sober party.

"You *what*?"

"I'll explain when you get here."

And I try to explain to them. I try to explain what happened. I tell them the story about Ozzy and the Pac-Man. But I can't really get the story right. The trouble is, when I tell it, it sounds like fun.

DAY 91

I AM WATCHING my fingers emptying out cigars and filling them with sticky green marijuana as if they belong to another person. I smoke joint after joint. I down glass after glass of red wine. My teeth turn red. My head spins. *Guess this is what they mean by a relapse!*

I can't work out whether I feel happy or sad. I know I felt happy for about the first five seconds, but now I am not so clear. What is happiness anyway?

I wander into another room and Alice is in there, crying. That's typical, that she should be there at the same party as me, like some guilty conscience. Her face is red and puffed up: "What are you doing Tom?" she sobs. "What the *fuck* are you doing?"

"Fuck you!" I shout at her and throw my glass at her. Her face melts into the wallpaper and I wander back into the main room. Everything has been moved around. I can't find the bar but a jumble of voices asks, "Fancy another one, Tom?!"

Why not! And another, and another! And then I am falling, falling, falling.

DAY 92

I WAKE UP the next afternoon, groaning in pain, racked with guilt, looking for the blood on my hands.

It takes a few seconds before I realise I haven't been anywhere. The whole thing has been a dream. I laugh like the maddest of the mad Port Authority drunks when I clock it. I have been warned about these "using dreams". I thought they might be fun. Not a nightmare, like that.

As I make my way to the bathroom, congratulating myself on the fact I haven't in fact been at a party the night before, I notice something very unexpected. I have a throbbing headache. It takes me just a few seconds to identify exactly what that oh-so-familiar sensation is.

I have a hangover.

I've lived a lifetime of good, bad and ugly, ugly, ugly hangovers. This phantom hangover is not one of the fun, innocent ones, where we had all crawled out of bed after a house party and fried sausages and bacon, sat round the kitchen table, swigging coffee, laughing at the previous night's outrageousness, smoking joints until it was time to go out again. Neither is it a suicide-inducing, lie-in-bed-and-don't-move number. It is just your regular, horrible, nothing-funny-about-that hangover. You know the kind – the dry mouth, the dull ache just underneath the crown of your head, the mossy tongue.

I figure that despite the fact I haven't been drinking I need to tackle this like it is any other hangover. I run a hot bath and I sit in it gulping iced water. I shave. I put on a Paul Smith shirt and a Kilgour suit. I cross the road to the noodle store and order a large bowl of extra spicy ramen, wash it down with Advil. I feel a little better. But just like a real hangover, it doesn't really leave me all day. My hangover cures, I belatedly realise, were all bullshit, because a hangover isn't just a headache or a sick stomach. A hangover is the physical expression of despair. And all the ramen and Advil in the world can't shift that.

A new guy walks in to the meeting that night. Says he wants to stop drinking. At the end of the meeting, I pounce on him, give him my number. I tell him to call anytime. I tell him I stay up late, late, late.

29

330 DAYS

THE DAYS TURNED into weeks, the weeks turned into months, and just before the months became a year Sasha got pregnant. Staying away from drink and drugs suddenly became more important than ever. So it was that I found myself sitting at my desk in my apartment in New York one Tuesday afternoon writing a list of my "resentments" – all the people I hated and why I hated them. This, I had been assured by my sober friends, would help me stay clean.

"Dad," I wrote, at the top of my list. "He abandoned me when I was fourteen. Never calls to see how I am, I always have to call him. Never in contact with me for sixteen years since then, unless I initiate it. Never explained why he left."

I dropped my pencil and rubbed my eyes in despair. This was useless. I already knew I resented my dad for having left my family. This was the *great trauma* of my life, after all.

And it wasn't like I was the one at fault. I had made an effort to see my father once or twice a year. When people asked why I bothered, I would tell them that it was so when he eventually died I would be able to go to his funeral with a clear conscience. But really, I knew, it was just because I liked hanging out with my dad. I could bask happily for hours in his intelligence, his wit and his charm. It was fun, as long as I didn't expect any answers, as long as I didn't say, "Why, Dad? Why did you do it?"

Well, now that was going to change. I got up from my desk and went into the other room to find my telephone book. I opened it to "S" and found his number, under "Mark Sykes". I went back to my desk and dialled it.

"Hello?"

'Hi, Dad. It's Tom."

"Tom! Hello there."

We chatted for a few minutes and then I screwed up my eyes, took a deep breath and asked, "So Dad, I am calling because I want to see you. I've got some questions I need to ask you."

"Right…" he said.

"Well," I said, "It's been sixteen years since you and Mum separated and, you know, it's ridiculous we can't talk about it. I need to ask you about it."

"Of course," said Dad. "Any time."

"Well, how about now?" I asked.

"Now?" he said incredulously. "No, I don't think so. Not over the phone. But maybe we could get together next time you are over?"

"OK," I said. "It shouldn't be too long."

I hung up the phone, logged on to the internet and booked a flight back to London for the weekend.

I emailed Dad right away. "How about next Tuesday?"

He shot back, "Fine. Let's talk details nearer the time."

DAY 337

THE FOLLOWING TUESDAY was drab and grey in England. I followed my dad's instructions through winding village lanes to a pub in rural Oxfordshire a few miles from where he was living. As I drove through the countryside in my rental car to meet him I wondered what the hell I was doing. What was I hoping to achieve? I prayed that at least I would have the courage to ask the questions that I had wanted to ask for so long, even if I didn't get any answers.

I was annoyed that Dad wanted to meet in a pub. I wanted to be somewhere private. I turned my car into the driveway of the bleak old stone pub and parked up. I was ten minutes early and Dad wasn't there yet.

I went inside and waited.

I ordered a Coke at the bar and wondered what he would say. I fantasised that he would choke up in tears and say, "Well, the thing was, Tom, I wanted to see you so much, but I had a nervous breakdown and I felt so guilty I just couldn't do it." Then I would start to cry as well and he would throw his arms around me and sob, "I'm sorry. I'm so sorry," and then I could forgive him.

I shook my head in disgust at myself. *You still think he can wave a magic wand, say the right thing and make it all better.* My hands were damp with sweat.

Bang on time, Dad pulled up outside. I watched him get out of the car and walk towards the pub. As he came through the door, I hugged him hello, as usual. He had a pint of lager and I stuck with my Coke. We engaged in ten minutes of the usual desultory chat.

"I really like gloomy pubs like this," he said. "The gloomier, the better."

"You would have loved this place Siberia," I said.

Dad finished his drink and said, "Right, come on. Let's go."

"Where?" I asked.

"I have arranged a delicious luncheon at my house," he said.

I grinned. Maybe we were going to have this conversation after all. I got in my car and followed him to a quaint stone village where he was living in a converted stable in someone else's garden.

"My business associates keep telling me I should move somewhere grander, somewhere with a dining room, but I like it here," he said, unconvincingly, as he let me in. There was a sitting room, with a coal fire going in the fireplace, two bedrooms off to the side and a virtually unused kitchen with a table littered with prescription drugs. In the sitting room, by the fire, there was a table covered in cold meats like chorizo and smoked salmon.

"There's also an attic room with dead bats in it," Dad laughed. He asked me whether I wanted Pellegrino to drink. As he opened the door of the fridge I noticed it was stuffed with about a dozen bottles of champagne. Dad always drank champagne.

"Enough champagne?" I asked.

"One always likes to keep a little on hand in case of emergencies," he chuckled.

In the main room, my eye was immediately drawn to the paintings on the walls. I recognised them from my childhood – a pair of elegantly framed, oval-shaped oils of some Sykes ancestors, a big gold picture of a Chinese man, a boy on a horse. I could picture the boy on the horse in the sitting room twenty years ago.

We sat down to lunch. I kept sneaking glances at my father across the table. He looked pretty good, but puffy around the cheeks and ears. He told me that he was taking steroids for an inflammatory condition he had developed. The previous Christmas he had been so badly immobilised he couldn't even get out of bed. His wife, Sandy, "The Fourth Mrs Sykes", as he called her, had had to come down to Oxfordshire from London, where she lived, to help him. The steroids had fixed all the immobility, but they were causing "terrible mood swings".

"Why do you and Sandy live apart?" I asked.

"She prefers it in London and I prefer it in the country," he said.

We chewed chorizo in silence for a little bit, until, eventually, I said, "So, I want to ask you some questions."

"If you look in the fire there, you will see that there are two potatoes wrapped up in tinfoil baking away."

"When did you put them in?" I asked.

"Before I went out. About thirty-five minutes ago."

"I don't think they'll be done yet, Dad," I said, then, before he could divert me again, I asked him how much he drank.

"Well, I don't normally drink in the day. Today is different, but of course *many* days are different," he laughed. "In the evening I would have the equivalent of a couple of beers and half a bottle of wine. And that's not a lot. I don't think. Maybe that would sometimes slip over into two-thirds of a bottle."

I asked him if he considered himself an alcoholic, and he replied, "Certainly not. Of course, I have frequently drunk far, far, far too much on a regular basis. But if you don't *need* a drink before ten in the morning you are *perfectly* all right."

I remembered when I thought that was what an alcoholic was – someone who had to have a drink in the morning. Over the past year, I've heard a better definition; that an alcoholic is someone who, once they have one drink, develops an overpowering craving for another. Now I see that is what always separated me from Sasha. She could stop.

Dad's tone was light and flippant, and he was starting to relax. I quizzed him further about his alcohol consumption, and about the drinking habit in our family. Easy stuff. Then I moved up an emotional gear.

"I came over especially to see you," I said, my heart beating faster.

"I also cancelled something," he said, "I was going to go to Baghdad this week to take part in a debate about Iraq."

I raised my eyebrows inquisitively. "Iraq?"

"I do want to go there," he said. "It's such a great opportunity to see chaos. Chaos is good, isn't it?"

I didn't have a chance to answer, "I saw some horrendous things in Algeria in the late Fifties. The things the French Foreign Legion did. Atrocities, atrocities, atrocities," he sighed.

I remembered this story from my childhood. My mind travelled back to that night when my dad had told me and Alice how he had seen babies speared by bayonets to the door frames of every house in an Algerian town. We had both burst into tears.

"It was 1957 and I was twenty," Dad continued. "I had dropped out of Oxford, and I started a club in London called the Whisky a Go-Go, which is still around. It's called the Wag. We opened this club for £4,000. It was an unbelievable success and we got the money back in two weeks.

"By the time I was twenty-two years old I had all this *money*. I went to Tangier. I got this job – not that I needed a job but I got one anyway – as a gopher for the *Time-Life* people there, covering the Algerian war. We saw the dead babies. That was in 1959."

He paused frequently as he relayed his potted life story to sip from his glass of wine. "In 1962 I was living in Paris, with my first wife, Helen. I went to Australia with her in '63 and '64, and I made a lot of money in Australia in the illegal gambling business. That's what I was doing in London before I left. I controlled all the illegal gambling in Australia. We were doing it in a classy way, with nice girls, nice food, all that sort of stuff."

"When did you marry Mum?"

"We got married in 1968. Shortly after all this."

"And you were happy for quite a long time, right?" I asked.

"I should think we were basically happy until the money ran out," he said, "Because money, make no mistake about it, money is unbelievably important. It doesn't matter when you have got it. It certainly does when you don't have it."

And then, suddenly, it went quiet and I squeezed all my courage into a ball in my chest.

"Look, Dad," I said, "Sixteen years down the line, I don't care why you and mum separated. That's between you and her ..."

"If you want a baked potato you will see a pair of tongs there ..."

"Er, OK." *If I don't have the courage to ask this, nothing will ever change.*

"What I was really wondering is why I never heard from you for so long. One moment you were this amazing dad and the next…"

Dad was ready. "I was asked to stay out of it. I was told it would be a very bad thing if I stuck my nose in and communicated with you and quite wrongly I accepted this."

At that moment my mobile phone went off. I cursed as I dug it out and switched it off.

"Potato?" my dad asked.

"I don't think they are ready yet," I said.

"OK, well, I am going to leave that up to you," he said.

I pressed on. "What about Fred and Josh? Don't you ever want to know what's going on with them?"

"I don't think it's my place to initiate things. I don't. Because I said I wouldn't. If something is initiated then wow, fantastic," he said.

I've been initiating contact for sixteen years. Why didn't you call me on that payphone at Eton when I was fifteen?

Then he said, "There's something else which I want you to tuck away at the back of your mind. When I die, my affairs are reasonably complicated. My will is going be lodged at the Central Registry of Wills and I am going to be making you the executor."

I paused, wondering how much my dad might be worth, then cursed myself for the thought.

But one thing about my father's eventual death had been bothering me for years. Now seemed a perfect opportunity to ask it. "When you die, how will I find out?" I asked.

He repeated slowly, "Central Registry of Wills, OK. It's all there."

"Yes," I said, irritated that he thought I hadn't understood. "But how will I know you are actually *dead*?"

"How will you know I am dead?" My dad roared with laughter. "Well, I suppose it is quite possible someone could find me here…" He pulled a death-mask face, groaned and sat back in his chair with his limbs starfished, simulating rigor mortis.

"But shouldn't your lawyer have my phone number?" I asked.

"Well, yes," my dad said, "But how would my lawyer know I was dead?"

We both laughed. Then there was more silence.

Eventually, I said, "So you were told, 'Stay away' and you stayed away? That's it?"

"Yes."

This must have been the first and last time Dad ever did what he was told. I said, "Weren't you curious though?"

"Yes, of course. But what's the point in being curious about something if you aren't going to have an answer? And, you know, I had so many *things* – some good and some bad – passing. Like getting cancer twice, which was very tiresome and quite death-inducing. Like building one amazing business, selling it and suddenly being a couple of *million* ahead. I thought, 'If I whack out a million quid among those children that might make a difference.' And then – boom! – like that, it was all gone.

In that fucking crash. However, I've done it again. At my advanced age." My dad sat back in his chair and smiled with smug satisfaction.

I tried to process the information. Was my dad *really* saying that between the start-up and the cancer he didn't have time to care about his six kids?

I tried again. "The thing that upsets me is that you were never in contact with us," I said, "And you say that is because you had ... other exciting stuff going on in your life?"

"Well, not necessarily exciting but occupying all of one's attention."

"But the shit that I went through from the time you went off to the time I left home!" I said. "Mum was so ill. And one day you were around – and you were this amazing, funny, wonderful dad, and the next you just weren't even there..."

"Well there we are," he said. "I regret that. I regret that. I regret that."

Another space opened up. *There. He said it. It's over. Walk away.*

There was another interminable pause and then he said, "Sadly we can't roll back the carpet."

Another even longer pause. Christ, this was like being in a Samuel Beckett play. Then he said, "Don't forget your fucking potato."

DAY 350

I GOT BACK to New York and spent the next two freezing winter weeks in a daze, trying to make sense of my meeting with Dad, but there was nothing to make sense of. Nothing had changed. Nothing had been resolved. The words of the psychiatrist I had seen at Eton all those years ago kept ringing in my ears: "I can't just wave a magic wand and make all of this disappear." He was right. My dad was right. What's the point in being curious about something if you aren't going to have an answer?

I went to see Plum one afternoon while I was trying to work out how I felt. She had a new apartment in Greenwich Village. There was a fire crackling in the grate, and she made a cup of tea, and asked how it went with Dad. What did I find out?

"Not much," I say. I stare intently into my tea cup. I feel stupid. What a waste of time. What a waste of seven hundred dollars.

The log in the fire pops. And then Plum says something which completely blows my mind. She says, "I think it was a good thing that Dad left."

"What?" I say, baffled. *This is my great tragedy.*

"Yes," says Plum, sitting up now, cross-legged in her armchair, focused, holding her cup of tea. "You know how everyone said it was so unfortunate and so sad at the time?"

I nod dumbly.

"Well, privately, between themselves, some of them said to each other, 'Thank God that man has left Valerie and the children at last.'"

"What?" The world shifts under my feet. It feels like an ice floe breaking up, or an earthquake cracking and resculpting the crust of the earth.

"Well, think about it Tom," said Plum. "Do you really think it would have been a good thing for you to continue to be influenced by Dad? With his dishonesty, his affairs, his drinking? Would you be a writer? Would you be who you are? Would you be sober?"

"I don't know," I say. I stare at the shapes of the flames in the grate for ten seconds. Then I say, "Plum, I've got to go. I'm sorry. I'll call you later."

I actually feel sick as I get into the elevator. It takes an eternity for the doors to close. I walk down to the subway station and get the train home. I want to throw up because the world is spinning like it used to when I was drunk.

As I rattle up to 55th Street I look back on my life and that familiar, well-rehearsed story suddenly looks so different. It's like that moment when you are looking at a hologram, and you shift your head just a few degrees and a whole new picture emerges. And it's not magic, it's just down to the way you are looking at it.

I think it was a good thing Dad left.

Plum might be right. Something I have always labelled "Bad Thing" might actually be a good thing. Or maybe it's not even a good thing. Maybe it's just something that happened, and that's just the way it is, and now it's time to get on with the rest of my life.

30

395 DAYS

I AM NOT A REGULAR visitor at the offices of the *New York Post* any more. There's a new bar columnist, fresh-faced nightlife writers. I still contribute items to *Page Six*, but I've stopped working regular shifts there. I invent excuses to swing by and catch up with Chris and Paula whenever I can, though, because I miss them. I miss my old life. I miss getting drunk. I miss the exhilaration of losing control, the drama, the craziness, the screaming on the streets, the cabs and the cops and the guns.

I went in one Wednesday, exactly fourteen months to the day after my second day zero. My excuse was that I needed to pick up my mail. I didn't. I could tell by the branding on the outside of the envelopes what most of it was. A new vodka, a new bar, a launch party. I slid the whole lot into the trash unopened.

"So what's going on?" said Chris.

"I'm heading back to Ireland tomorrow to catch up with Sasha," I said. "She went ahead yesterday."

"You're going away *again*?" asked Chris.

"Well, yeah. We're planning to spend a few months in Ireland once the baby comes. We want to try and rent a farmhouse for the summer where we could live."

Sasha was seven months pregnant now.

"You're going to go and live in *Ireland*?" Chris asked as his phone began to ring.

"Just for a few months," I replied, defensively. "We're keeping the apartment here."

"So, you're leaving tomorrow," Chris stated. It wasn't a question. Both lines on his phone were ringing now.

Then I blurted out, "Hey, you want to go out tonight? Siberia?"

"Yeah, sure," said Chris, picking up his phone and putting his palm over the mouthpiece. "I have some big news to tell you."

"What?"

"It's big, man," laughed Chris. "Believe me, it's huge."

"I'll call you at around ten," I mouthed, and headed off down the corridor in the direction of the elevator as he started talking on the phone.

Chris rang me at about 9.45. He was at a mutual friend's house in Greenwich Village having dinner. Did I want to come over? We could head out from there.

I jumped in a cab and I let myself slide from side to side in the back on the way there. I tried not to think about how stupid I was being. My mouth was watering every time I thought of a drink, the dry kick of a vodka, the satisfying bouquet of a glass of red wine.

Stop it, I thought to myself. *You're not going to drink and that's that.* But surely I *had* to be able to go into bars and clubs safely now. I had fourteen months sober. I'd been into a few bars in the past year, but never for much longer than I could avoid – half an hour or so max. Tonight was going to be a marathon in comparison.

The dinner party was in full swing when I arrived at the stylish and sumptuous two-storey apartment on 6th Avenue. There were eight people there, and dessert – olive oil ice-cream delivered from Otto, a fancy Italian restaurant round the corner – was just being served. Most of the guests were still sitting around the large, wooden farmhouse table under a spiral staircase that led upstairs, but the focus of the party was shifting to a glass-topped coffee table at the other end of the room where a tall, pretty Russian dancer was chopping up some lines of cocaine on a glass table in front of an open fire.

"Vant a line?" she asked, all cheekbones and lips, as I walked in. It was the first thing anyone said to me. The coke looked kind of good, in an insane way, but Chris was already up out of his chair, coming towards me and replying for me. "No man, he doesn't do that shit anymore." He stood up to give me a hug. "Good to see you man."

Some of the guests started snorting lines. The host and hostess declined. Chris and I settled into the leather sofas around the fire. The host offered me a diet Coke. He had a load in his fridge.

"So what's the big news?" I asked Chris, as I poured Coke into a wine glass.

Chris smiled, took another sip on his glass of red wine, and smiled again. "You won't believe it man. I'm dating a stripper."

"That's it?" I asked. "I was expecting you to tell me – I dunno – that you had a new job or something."

"Man, you don't understand. This girl is a *Scores* stripper." He looked at me meaningfully. Scores was a chain of flashy lapdancing clubs in the city. "That means she is one of the hottest strippers in the world. And she is dating me."

Chris shook his head smugly. "I mean, it's *ridonculous* dude. We are different life forms. I'm a monkey and she is a goddess. She tans. She drinks juice. She has this perfect, flat belly. It's a model banging a monkey."

We hung around at the party till about midnight, by which time the host was ushering his guests out of the door. He wiped the coke crumbs off the table with an old cloth and a look of disdain. He saw me catch his expression, and said, "I mean, it's *Wednesday*."

He sat down next to me and sighed. "Don't you find drunk people really boring now?" he asked.

"Well, I don't hang around with them when they are actually *drunk* very much anymore," I said. "But yeah, it's kind of tedious sometimes. People high on coke are the worst. When someone who you hardly know gets on a coke-a-log and invites you on holiday, that's when it's time to leave."

He laughed. "Do you get tempted to drink?"

"Sometimes. But I don't really get tempted to drink at parties or bars anymore just because I think it would be fun. Now, I want to drink when I get scared."

I was thinking of the night before my grandmother's funeral a few months earlier, when I was staying in my brother Fred's room, and I got an alcohol craving in the night. I was feeling desperately guilty about how I had wasted all the house money my grandmother had left me. I had betrayed the one woman who had done more for me and my family than anyone else in the world, and now she was dead. I had to go and wake up my other brother Josh at three in the morning and get him to hide a bottle of whiskey that was sitting on the shelf of Fred's room.

"Maybe it's time for us to go as well," I said. "Chris, you ready?"

"Yeah man, let's go," he yelled, draining his wine glass. "Siberia, one last time. Who's coming?"

It was just the two of us.

Still, it was fun, riding up town with Chris wise-cracking all the way, boasting about his new girlfriend and then rocketing out of the cab when we got to our destination so he didn't have to pay the fare. Just like old times, I thought, as I paid up and asked for a receipt.

Siberia was exactly the way it was when I left. The floor was the texture of molasses. Nirvana was blasting out of the jukebox. Patrick was still behind the bar. One difference was a brand new pinball machine winking away where the Pac-Man I had demolished fourteen months earlier once stood.

"So, you got a new pinball machine," I said to Gareth, an Irish guy who sometimes worked for Tracey at Siberia as an electrician. He was a regular but he didn't remember me.

"Oh yeah," Gareth said. "It's only about two weeks old that one. The old one got smashed."

I frowned. Hang on, this was a new *new* pinball machine?

"How did the other one get smashed?" I asked.

"Well, it involved a lot of drink," Gareth said, speaking frenetically. "A big, hairy man threw a cash register at the wall, that wall over there, and it was going so fast that it ricocheted off and hit the glass. But, it was, like, safety glass, so it didn't smash properly, so he went over and smashed it up with his head." Gareth smiled.

"A big hairy man?" I asked in disbelief. "Tracey? Tracey smashed up his *own* pinball machine in his *own* bar? That's pure Siberia."

"You see man?" exclaimed Chris, swigging on a beer. "You see how little it matters what you did smashing up that Pac-Man? Personally, I was like, 'Big deal,' but *you* took it as a sign from God. You were totally premature."

We were standing by the bar when Tracey walked in, at about half past midnight, with his son.

We walked to the back of the bar and sat on two leather sofas set at right angles to each other. There were no more than six other people in the bar – Chris, Gareth and another former barman, Kieran, who had come in with a few girls who were hanging around by the Harleys.

"So I heard you got sober," Tracey said, right away. "You're a better man than most and I hope when it's my turn I am man enough to quit."

"Thanks Tracey," I muttered. I always get embarrassed when people congratulate me on my sobriety. Firstly, I feel that I didn't really have much to do with it, that it just kind of happened, and secondly, I worry about that being one more person to laugh at me if I ever drink again.

"Was I really bad? Even by Siberia standards?" I asked him.

"Look man," said Tracey, "I run another bar round the corner called Bellevue. That's named after the city psych ward. We have people who show up there asking for Dr Katz. We don't deal with dead-on knuckleheads, but you were pretty far out there."

"And the night I smashed up the Pac-Man? What did you think then?"

Tracey pulled on his goatee and considered his answer carefully. "That thing was there for nine years. And you were the only person to break it. So you've got to figure first" – he pushed his right thumb into his left palm – "First, it's not very easy to break and second" – he marked the point with his index finger – "Second, how far out have you got to be to do something like that? So it's good you chilled the fuck out because you could do something to hurt some-one or yourself. Most likely yourself."

As Tracey was chatting, we were suddenly enveloped by a strong petro-chemical smell.

Tracey leapt up out of the sofa with amazing alacrity given his massive bulk and yelled, "Who's spraying shit in here?"

Gareth was standing by the Harleys looking guilty. "Someone knocked over the Harley," he said. "And gas came out."

"It's not supposed to having fucking gas in it!" yelled Tracey. Then he turned to me. "I've got my son with me. We've got to get out of here. I'm not about to get crisped in a bar with my son."

We went outside with Chris and Gareth. I had a cigarette while Tracey carried on talking about my drinking. "The thing is, Tom, I'd see you hit that switch and just go into another world. You just went over the edge," he said.

"I'm really sorry about the Pac-Man," I said. "Do I owe you for it?"

"What you can do for me is give your wife a kiss and stay away from the whiskey. That's your payback to me. Come on, let's go to Bellevue and let the fumes clear out."

An hour or so later Chris and I were sitting at the counter in the bar next door to Bellevue. I asked him, "So, when are you going to give up drinking man?"

"When I die," said Chris, and slugged back his vodka and tonic. "I can't imagine a life without alcohol. I can't give it up ever."

It was 1.30am. "I miss you," he said. "You were one of my best friends, and we were just raging … animals. I thought I loved this guy and he's gone. I miss you man."

"I miss you too, Chris," I said, shaking my head. "I miss it all."

It was the truth. I don't want to go back there, but I miss it. "You know what I miss most?" I asked him. "I miss the never quite knowing what is going to happen or where you're going to end up."

We sat in silence for a few more moments.

"Let's get out of here," I said.

We headed for the door and stood on the pavement for a few moments.

"Wanna go to Bungalow?" said Chris after a few seconds.

"Bungalow? I dunno. You're kind of wasted ..."

Chris came up close to me, his face within inches of my own. "This is what we used to be like all the time, bro," he shouted.

"There is that, I guess," I said. "Let's go."

We got into a cab but as we were speeding down 9th Avenue, Chris said, "If we go to Marquee we'll get our own table and bottles. Shall we do Marquee instead?"

"OK," I said. "You think they'll let you in?"

"Of course man! I'll just walk to the front of the line and go, 'Yo! Richie! What's up?' And BAM! We'll go straight in."

We pulled up outside Marquee and Chris pulled open the street-side door and climbed out. The taxi driver started to yell at him to get out the other side but Chris just muttered, "I'll cut your throat."

I paid the cab and Chris and I walked to the front of the line. As Chris had predicted we said, "Yo! Ritchie! What's up?" and went right in.

Noah Tepperberg, the owner of the club, was waiting for us when we walked in. He was always there when you walked in because he spent the night watching the door line on CCTV in a side office radioing instructions to the doorman on which wannabes to let in and who to bounce.

He hugged me hello, then shouted over the booming sound system: "You guys want a table?"

"Sure," shouted Chris, and we followed Noah to one of the prized tables in the centre of the club. The space was packed with its usual clientele – the stunning twenty-four-year-old girls, rappers and rich bankers dressed in suits. A lithe waitress brought over a bottle of vodka and an ice bucket filled with champagne and beer and set them on the low table in front of us. I ordered a glass of Coke.

"You want anything else, let me know," she said, flashed us a mile-wide smile and disappeared back into the writhing crowd. There would be no bill tonight. Not for *Page Six*.

The bottle whores began swarming our table in search of a free drink. We handed out beers and champagne and vodka cranberries. Chris had been playfighting all night but now the punches were starting to get just a little harder. I noticed a smartly dressed, blond guy in a suit and tie standing by our table, following me and Chris wherever we went. Who was this dude?

I went and sat down on the back of the banquette at our table with my feet on the seat. Noah came up and sat next to me. We chatted for a bit, then I said, "Who's that blond guy who keeps following us around?"

Noah laughed and said, "That's Chris's security detail."

"What?" I said.

"I have a security guard to tail him to make sure he doesn't hurt himself," said Noah, as Chris started laying into Paolo Zampolli, the head of ID models, pushing and play-punching him way too hard.

Then I said, "Noah, did you used to get a security guard to tail me when I was in here?"

"Sure," he said. "You and Chris needed it man."

"And you do all that, put up with all that shit, gave me all that licence just because I worked on *Page Six*?" Paolo Zampolli was fighting his way across the dance floor away from Chris. In fact, a space had opened up in a four-foot radius around Chris, the only space in the entire club, which was rammed. It reminded me of when you think you've miraculously found a seat on a crowded tube train but when you get there, there's vomit on the floor.

Noah flinched. "Not just because of *Page Six* but because you and Chris are my buddies," he said, looking hurt. "All the press get some licence but Chris and you are friends. So you always got this special treatment. Still do."

Chris was standing at the table, pouring himself another vodka with painstaking attention, glass and bottle both at eye level. Noah started ordering some more drinks from the hostess for the table.

"Do you want something Tom?"

"Just another diet Coke please Noah," I said. Then I looked at my watch. It was three am. I didn't need another diet Coke. It was way, way past time for me to go as it was. "Actually, forget it, I'm fine," I said.

I went over to Chris, gave him a hug and said, "Look after yourself mate. I've got to go."

"I love you man," he slurred. We hugged. "This is it, man. I'm never going to see you again."

"Of course we'll see each other again," I said. But I knew what he meant. The Tom Sykes he was talking about was last seen demolishing a Pac-Man fourteen months ago in Siberia.

I got my coat and left Marquee for the last time.

It was cold outside, and it felt good to be in the fresh air. My head felt thick and heavy from the music, the smoke and the dancing. I could guarantee I would have a phantom hangover tomorrow.

There was still a mob of two hundred or so people desperate to get into Marquee and take my place. They were coming up with all the lines.

"My boyfriend's inside ..."

"Noah's expecting me ..."

"We've got a table reservation ..."

"I just came out for a cigarette ..."

Nightlife is big business. Casualties like me, well, we're just natural wastage.

396 DAYS

I'M IN A CAB on the way to the airport the next afternoon, looking forward to seeing Sasha and wondering what sex our baby will be and realising I don't care just, please God, let it be healthy. My phone rings. It's Chris.

I pick up. "Wilson?"

"Mr Sykes," he says, his voice crackly and dry and hungover.

"How are you?" I ask.

"Oh my god," he croaks. "I have just one question for you. What did I do last night?"

THE END